Sandy Andrew's book *Your Never*  at
brilliantly explains Universal Law: f
the Universe. Sandy's book is the ke
and how to apply this wisdom to li
life. A must-read for everyone! ...g

Barbara Gulbranson
www.barbaragulbranson.com

Finally, a book providing a simplified cornerstone for understanding
our purpose on earth, and how to attune to Universal Energy by
absorption utilizing 12 Universal Laws. Universal Learning reveals
how we reason on the spiritual and emotional levels. Included in the
exceptional work is exploration of questions and belief systems related
to religion and truth.

Bernie P. Nelson
www.lightwordreviews.com

Sandy Andrew, like most New Age thinkers, takes a very inclusive
approach to spirituality, and urges tolerance towards other's beliefs:
surely a much needed thing in these troubled times. He believes that
we are all free to choose whatever religion we please, and that there
are many paths to ultimate spiritual fulfillment. He does embrace the
language and belief system of a creator God, but his God seems more
to be a loving father than a fire and brimstone type, and, as mentioned,
he includes eastern concepts such as the law of karma.

Bodhipaksa - Wildmind Buddhist Meditation
www.wildmind.org

The thought of reincarnation escapes most people, as it did me until
I read this book. Sandy does a wonderful job of laying foundations,
and then carefully explaining those feelings we have all had in our lives.
When you're finished with his book, written in a warm and unassaulting
style, you may know yourself a little better. But you most certainly will
be convinced that you have existed for many thousands of years and
have relished the beauty and sadness in all your lives. The greatness

in the lives of mankind is the fruit of spiritual debts paid and loves cherished over the eternities. And we're nowhere near complete with our journey. Search your higher mind, find your soul mate, and know that you are never alone in this world. Sandy has discovered for us a treasure.

Brooks A. Agnew, PhD
www.x2-radio.com

These days, there is no shortage of spiritual guidebooks on bookstore shelves. From Nubian extraterrestrial cults to pagan Celtic ritual, authors are resuscitating (or inventing) mystical lifeways. And though many possess capable intellect and present intriguing ideas, few works are compelling enough to stand apart from the pack. In contrast, Sandy Andrew's *Your-Never Ending Life* is a remarkable piece of prose—as well-written as it is informative.

An ambitious text addressing the sorts of broad themes and questions that send parents and pastors running for cover, Andrew's treatment is a masterpiece of simplicity that belies the depth of the concepts within. With clarity and vigor, Andrew describes "universal learning" and provides tools for readers to begin to understand and practice this essential act.

Of course, mention of extra dimensions, universal energy, and spiritual beings sets off the "New Age" alarm. The charming thing about Andrew is that he accepts this moniker and even self-labels his work as being such. He unabashedly presents his views, views which are, though radical, well-thought and meticulously argued.

Your-Never Ending Life: Book 1 of the Universal Learning Series is a must-read for anyone interested in understanding the purpose of life—which makes this extraordinary work a must-read for everyone, regardless of age, nationality, or faith. If there were more Sandy Andrew's in the world, humanity would be much improved. Too bad this author is such a stunning original.

By New York Times Best Selling Author Ellen Tanner Marsh

Mr. Andrew has captured an understanding of our place in God's creation without dogma. This alone leaves you refreshed and hopeful of a better tomorrow.

Ernie Vecchio
www.innerscape.org

Sandy has written a book that is easy for anyone to believe in and understand. He explains the 12 Laws that are important for anyone who wishes to manifest and live a life of their own choosing, and he does it in such a way that regardless of your religious beliefs, you can still take heart and believe in the answers he has written in his book, the ones that answer your Questions about who you are, why you are here, and what is it you are here to do.

Frankie Picasso
www.instituteforquantumliving.com

Your Never-Ending Life is a remarkable spiritual text for the next step in the new age. Written for the enlightenment of the emerging technologically- minded generation, who have less time than ever and prefer their information
condensed into "bytes" of wisdom, Sandy Andrew has found his audience. His book explains the basic spiritual laws in easy-to-understand language and then teaches how to implement those laws into practical everyday use. He is a new-age writer for the future, and I would recommend this book as an introduction to the basic universal laws for anyone beginning their spiritual journey.

Georgia Slesinger
www.onelightpsychic.com

Most other books that I have read on this topic tend to only talk about the life energy between all living things or about the spiritual guidance of God. This has been the only book, thus so far, that I have read that emphasizes the importance of both. You see so much being said about adhering to a balance in life yet it seems so difficult at times to accept that there must also be a spiritual balance between how much you put into the hands of a higher being and how much you take into your own hands.

Jennifer Somerset
www.bookpleasures.com

I read Mr. Andrew's book with great interest as I too am interested in the universal energy field/force. I found this to be a book that I easily read from cover to cover and for me, all of it was enlightening and in complete agreement with my thoughts and feelings. I feel this book is a wonderful introduction into the study of universal energy and how to understand and work with that energy. Highly recommended.

Dr. John L. Turner
www.johnlturner.com

I greatly enjoyed reading *Your Never Ending Life* by Sandy Andrew. From a spiritual viewpoint and as a professional psychic counselor I found the guidance he offered much in sync with my own beliefs. You won't find any far out teachings or ways of thinking. You won't find any hard to understand or difficult to follow "rules." His ideas are solid and logical. From a reader's point of view I enjoyed the bite-sized entries.

Kelly Wallace
www.authorautobahn.com

Reading this book will bring the understanding of why we are here, and how we can make the changes that will bring us happiness, fulfillment and joy. It is a major work that is needed so desperately on this planet. In a time of chaos, this is a light in the window of your life. Read it and grow. I highly recommend it.

Leona Mayers
www.leonamayers.com

Sandy has tapped into the knowledge that all beings carry sleeping within them. When you read his book you will find yourself recognizing the truth rather than learning something new for the first time. The result could be for you what happened to me, a wonderful sense of joy and peace washing over me that hasn't left me since.

Robin Lamb
North Carolina, USA

Your Never-ending Life: Book 1 of the Universal Learning Series has brought his unique style of writing even further to the surface to enlighten the reader on such important matters as "What You Are", "The Universe and Energy", "The Path and Choices", and "Success or Failure", just to name a few. He has reached out and captured through his words and strong feeling the attention of the reader. He has also given examples, in plain view, of the universal laws for the reader to understand.

Wanda Maynard
www.simegen.com

Your Never-Ending Life

Book 1 of The Universal Learning Series

Sandy Andrew

iUniverse, Inc.
New York   Bloomington

Your Never-Ending Life
Book 1 of The Universal Learning Series

The views expressed in this work are solely those of the author and do not necessarily reflect the views of the publisher, and the publisher hereby disclaims any responsibility for them.

iUniverse books may be ordered through booksellers or by contacting:

iUniverse
1663 Liberty Drive
Bloomington, IN 47403
www.iuniverse.com
1-800-Authors (1-800-288-4677)

Because of the dynamic nature of the Internet, any Web addresses or links contained in this book may have changed since publication and may no longer be valid.

ISBN: 978-1-4401-8927-2 (sc)
ISBN: 978-1-4401-8928-9 (ebk)

Library of Congress Control Number: 2009912263

Printed in the United States of America

iUniverse rev. date: 1/13/2010

Your Never-Ending Life: Book 1 of The Universal Learning Series Published by The Universal Learning Series

Visit our website at www.universallearningseries.com

The work I have done here would not be possible without the guidance of the superior spirit, the one that created me, whom I love and honor, and will never deny.

Contents

Introduction

I wrote this *Book 1 of The Universal Learning Series* to inform the reader of the general concept of universal learning and how it relates to your lifetime on the planet Earth. This learning consists of human emotions and life experiences, which is the purpose of your lifetime on Earth. In this dimension, the universal learning is frame worked around twelve universal laws and the energy of the universe. The universal laws and energy guide our physical and spiritual existence in God's entire universe.

In my lifetime of experiencing emotions and events, I have learned that the universal laws and the energy of the universe which we all belong to are imperative in bringing success and fulfillment in our lifetimes. I have overcome many difficult obstacles and challenges, and even still do to this day, by harnessing the power of universal energy and by observing the universal laws. I have lived in four countries and three continents, from one side of the world to the other, and seen many great things. I have learned and achieved academically, socially, and culturally against all the odds by opening my mind to the concept of universal learning.

One of the benefits of universal learning is that it can be applied to any human being regardless of race, gender, or religious background, as you do not need to discard any faith that you currently have.

From this book, I desire to pass along to you, the reader, the knowledge that I carry and the hope that it will help you achieve a more successful and fulfilling lifetime on Earth.

I will explain to you who you really are, why you are here on planet Earth, and cover some fundamental principles in achieving success and fulfillment in your lifetime of universal learning.

Part 1

The Spirit—Who you are

The question, "Who am I?" has been asked by all human beings at least once in their life. In part one we shall discuss the universe and energy along with the universal laws. Followed by explaining what you are. We conclude part one with the concept of universal learning and why spirit needs to learn and grow.

Chapter 1

The Universe & Energy

The Universe

The Universe consists of infinite spiritual and living dimensions that are transcendent in scale. The spiritual dimensions are places like the heavens and other realms. An example of a living dimension is the Milky Way galaxy. You may think this galaxy is huge—and it is, but we have now estimated 125 billion other galaxies as well—interesting? You may wonder if there are 125 billion other dimensions that also exist. No, the Milky Way and the other 125 billion are all a part of one living dimension. You may think this is too big to comprehend; try to not compare the universe in size and scale to ordinary human knowledge and understanding. There are an infinite number of living dimensions in the universe just as there are in the spiritual dimensions.

Being transcendent in scale and having an infinite number of dimensions, the universe is somewhat difficult for us humans to comprehend, because it has no start, middle, or end. Although we can estimate when our living dimension was created, we cannot determine the date of birth of God's entire universe—and be advised, we never will.

God encourages discovery and exploration, as this facilitates learning and spiritual growth, but we will never know it all, and He will always keep mankind and other life forms in the living dimensions, guessing. In 2005, scientists discovered a new interesting theory in the formation of the Milky Way galaxy as the result of tests suggesting that the galaxy behaved like a liquid in its earliest moments, and not so much like the raging inferno of the Big Bang theory that we have been led to believe. You also recall that for decades we thought the galaxy was contracting only to find out that it's actually expanding!

In many New Age books, including this one, the term "universe" can have a dual meaning. So, let us clarify this to avoid confusion:

- In this living dimension, we use the term "living universe" to refer to outer space; the billions of other galaxies, including the Milky Way galaxy with its planets: Earth, Mars, and Pluto, for example.

- In a spiritual sense, it refers to the angels, guides, and endless heavenly spiritual dimensions. The phrase "working with the universe," can mean working with the guides. There is no time measurement in the spiritual dimension. The term "universal learning" means to learn "God's ways".

Energy

The infinite universe and all of its contents, whether it be the living or spiritual dimensions, are classified as forms of energy— all of it. That means our homes, cars and human bodies. Heaven, your spirit, your thoughts, and even God are forms of energy.

In the living dimension, many things appear solid to our physical senses, but are simply made up of billions of atoms. All physical substances are forms of energy, because they have relationships at the atomic and sub-atomic levels.

Two examples of energy in the living dimension:

- Consider a star, which is a mass of energy. (For example: Our Sun is a source of energy for our planet Earth.)

- Consider a slab of natural rock, people may say that is as "solid as a rock" and contains no energy. Oh really? Let's set the slab in a waterfall environment for 1000 years and let's see how much erosion has taken place. People may say, "Oh that is too long to wait!" There is no time in the spiritual dimension and we can incarnate back into the physical world as a life form to inspect the slab of rock.

Energy vibrates at different speeds. Things such as a rock and a wooden chair are examples of slow moving energy, and a speeding car and electricity are examples of fast moving energy. You may ask the question: "Is a stationary car classified as energy too?" If we took a stationary car and melted it down, it would convert to a molten state; then a conversion of potential energy would have taken place.

Two examples of energy in the spiritual dimension are:

- Your spirit
- The afterworld dimension—heaven is an entire, endless dimension, which is merely another form of energy

In this spiritual dimension, we often refer to energy in relation to many things, such as meditation and emotions, for example. You will hear many spiritual teachers refer to centering, grounding, and running energy. You may wonder what the blazes they are talking about. Energy is the life force of all the universal dimensions and is the endless fuel supply that feeds and controls everything. The term "running energy," for example, means allowing your higher mind to access the flow of universal energy that is present in your dimension, which allows it to flow through your body. This concept may seem a little spooky to some, but you subconsciously do it all the time, and you can also access this energy flow easily through simple meditation.

By the nature of your very existence as a creation of God, you are connected to the universe at all times. Sudden thoughts that enter into your conscious are from your own higher mind and spiritual guides, which pass on messages of guidance to you in the form of spiritual energy, which your earthly conscience processes as normal thoughts and intuition.

Your thoughts emanate an energy field, your emotions emanate an energy field, and your spirit is an energy field— there is no escaping the energy fields. Energy fields can manifest themselves into reality, therefore the saying "Be careful what you wish for as you may get it", is most true. Have you ever walked into a room and sensed a peculiar atmosphere, although no one has even spoken a word? You are sensing a negative or even a positive energy field. People's thoughts emanate an energy field and your higher mind sometimes senses it very accurately. This is when, for example, you hear people say, "You could have cut the atmosphere with a knife in there."

There is positive and negative energy in the universe. On an emotional level, examples of positive energy are love, compassion, kindness, and empathy. Anger, fear, hate, and bitterness are examples of negative energy. In the living dimension, we need a negative to balance the positive energy. However, in the spiritual dimensions there is only positive energy. You may ask why this is so. Well, if there was only positive energy in the living dimension, how could we possibly learn? Everything would be harmonious bliss and you would not be faced with all the scenarios and decisions that facilitate growth of the spirit

We will discuss, in more detail, accessing the flow of universal energy in chapter 11; Inner Guidance.

Chapter 2

The Universal Laws

These are a set of rules that guide our universal existence, which include both the spiritual and living dimensions. While incarnated in this living dimension, we must try to follow twelve simple guidelines from the universal laws which pertain to this world and those spirits incarnated as human beings in a lifetime of universal learning.

The universal laws are not a set of cast-iron rules which, if broken, will cause you to be thrown into a pit of flames in the afterworld for some errors of judgment you have made in your lifetime. As you will ascertain further on in the book, the laws are nothing too complicated: they are merely the framework for understanding the events that seem to unfold in our lifetimes. You have the free will to make all the choices in your life, yourself (except for times of warfare and some exceptional circumstances). You are responsible for your own lifetime on Earth. The universal laws are meant to guide the spirit and if they are followed, your lifetime and existence will be more balanced, loving, and fulfilled, for the most part. No lifetime is perfect and each lifetime will have its challenges, highs, and lows; albeit at different intensities.

Observing these laws can assist you to truly achieve spiritual growth, which is the essence of your existence and the reason why you are here on Earth. The harsh reality is that the more you break and fight against these laws, the tougher you make this life and your future lifetimes to follow. You are allowed to make errors in judgment, as none of us are perfect, but all universal actions and karmic debts have to be repaid; hence a lifetime to relearn a lesson.

The twelve particular universal laws that we focus on in this book are our guidelines from God that set the format of our existence as a spirit currently participating in universal learning on Earth. You may think you are a hotshot know it all, or extremely wealthy and above this, but you will pass from this world one day and you will have to account for the decisions and actions you undertook during your lifetime. No one is exempt from the universal laws. You will find yourself leading meaningful, fulfilling, but nonetheless, still challenging lives, if you pay heed the universal laws. When you clash against them, then you may find the journey goes from bad to downright terrible. Review these laws and let your higher mind absorb and remember the information. When you face choices in life, you can recall these laws to guide your decisions.

An analogy of the universal laws to present day life is when you go to your job or go about your daily business, the laws of the land do not tell you how to do your job, or how to live your life, however, they do state the rules and guidelines that you must stay within. The universal laws are no different; as you come to Earth, to live and learn, the laws are the guidelines to observe and stay within.

Listed are the twelve universal laws that pertain to spirits who are at this stage of their universal learning—quite simply, this is to anyone reading this book. Be advised, there are many universal laws that are not relative to this dimension and a lifetime on Earth.

1. Karma
2. Love
3. Emotional Control
4. Action & Effect
5. Preordination
6. Incarnation Characteristic

7. **Protection**
8. **Time**
9. **Guidance**
10. **Learning**
11. **Restoration**
12. **Free Will**

1. Karma

The karma law is simple to understand: as you do, so shall it be done to you. As you sow, then so shall you reap. What goes around comes around. In simple terms, you will get out of life what you put into it.

Examples of the law of karma:

- In your marriage or relationship; you commit an unfaithful act towards your partner. The same or equivalent will be dealt towards you, whether in this lifetime, or the next.

- You commit an unjustifiable murder in this lifetime; therefore, you will experience an equal fate in this or another life. The karmic debt you owe will be repaid in one form or another.

I must state though that you are here to learn, and you will make mistakes; we all do. You must truly learn from your mistakes and be aware that all Karmic debts will be repaid, meaning for every ounce of hateful acts you unjustifiably served on another spirit, so shall the same be done to you.

When you hear people say, "what goes around comes around," this is where they get it from; the universal law of karma. Make no mistake; I can assure you what ever you do to another in a lifetime will come right back at you, no matter whom you think you are in this world.

2. Love

The law of love can be interpreted in different ways, but overall it means to show affection for a person or thing. Love is the most beautiful and powerful emotion there is. The saying, "Love conquers all," is most true.

Consider this example:

- Have you ever seen the movie *The Passion of the Christ?* You recall the brutal whipping and lashing scenes? Ask yourself this question, "Would you wish that extremely harsh treatment on your worst enemy?" You may think, "I don't love my enemies in the same way I do my family and friends, or even my faith." No, but you love God, the universe, and all its spirits. Your answer to the question after deep thought and rationalization is probably "No, I don't want my enemy to experience this harsh treatment, but I do want justice under the law." You see, love conquers all.

To follow the guideline of the universal law of love all you need to do is to show some love and compassion in your life. Without love in your life, you will feel empty and hollow. The opposite emotion of love is hate, and as we have mentioned already, hate will lead to suffering for all concerned. Adherence to the law of love can only bring happiness and fulfillment in your life.

Forgiveness is part of the law of love. You learn to forgive as a result of your love for the universe—believe it or not. You do not have to interact, or walk up in the street and hug those who have hurt you in your life, but you need to learn to forgive people and move on. Learn from the experience and use it for your future benefit. Forgiveness is a very important part of the law of love because so many events transpire during a lifetime that if we did not learn to forgive, our lives would be filled with hate and revenge, which are negative emotions. You cannot spiritually progress in your lifetime while you remain embroiled in negative emotions. Be advised, one way or the other universal justice will be done and karmic debts will be repaid by anyone who unjustifiably harms you.

It took me a long time in my life to forgive a few people for the way they treated me—old girlfriends, imagine that! My only regret is that I should have forgiven and forgot about them years ago and got all with my life in a more productive way. I say this because I know there are many of you reading this book that have had at relationship at one point in your life where someone has acted wrongly against you.

3. Emotional Control

This law involves controlling the positive and negative emotions. This is a pivotal law in your life, and it will determine your future. While you are here on Earth to participate in universal learning, which consists of emotional and life experiences, it is very important that you don't waste your energy on negative emotions.

For example:

- Completing a life experience, such as being a successful entrepreneur, must not be achieved by using fear, manipulation, or lies. This would result in you deluding yourself that you completed the life experience, when you failed, by utilizing negative emotions rather than positive ones.

We list some positive and negative emotions in more detail in chapter 6. At some point in your life, you will experience positive and negative emotions. You are allowed to experience the negative emotions in all lifetimes, but you must control them and not act on them to unjustifiably harm others. It is very important to adhere to the positive side of emotions and to not give in to the more negative ones which will cause you and others much unhappiness and suffering.

For example:

- Fear, which seems be the root of all negative emotions, takes hold of your life and dominates your thinking; you will only know negative results in most undertakings you embark on in life. Let's say you are about to take an academic examination and you're fraught with the fear of failing the exam. Your fear of failing will affect your performance in the exam and you will be unhappy about it.

Try your very best not to let negative emotions control and dominate your life. Sometimes we do not realize that fear and hate have entrenched themselves so much in our everyday thinking that it almost seems normal. Be advised our thoughts and intentions create energy fields which can manifest themselves into reality.

In my lifetime, I have learned to maintain control over my emotions. When I was younger I used to give in to fear and anger and ultimately the outcome of many situations were not so good. I found out, to my surprise, that faced again with the same situations I maintained control over my emotions and did not lash out and the situations were resolved satisfactorily.

4. Action & Effect

For very action there is a reaction. This law works closely with the law of Karma.

A few examples to review:

- You backstab a colleague to get a promotion and then in the future you get backstabbed. You caused the effect of the backstabbing by the effect of your actions in the first instance. The Law of Karma will dictate: you shall reap by what you sow. You sowed the seed of backstabbing and it flourished and came right back for you.

- Let's say, you eat too many chocolates and get an upset stomach, as well as gain body fat. The action was overeating and the effect was the physical feeling of not being well.

- You have unprotected sex and get pregnant. You caused this action by first having intercourse, and secondly, not taking any precautionary measures to avoid pregnancy.

- Someone is deliberately talking trash and trying to provoke you at work. You over-react and physically attack them. You lose your job and as result and have put yourself under huge financial strain. You chose to physically attack this person when some form of verbal response would have sufficed.

There is no action you can take, without a resulting effect. Think about the effect of your action prior to making a decision on anything.

In my lifetime I would not have been able to live in South Africa or the United States of America without the action of studying and working hard in order to gain the necessary credentials to bring about the effect of legal resident status.

5. Preordination

There will be events that will happen in your life no matter what. Sometimes these events are good, sometimes bad, but they are all learning experiences for us. Trust me. When the dust settles and you look back in life, you will view these sometimes-traumatic events with a clearer understanding.

An example of this:

- You may have to experience an event of grief and sadness. You lose a dear loved one and you have to come to terms with it, in due time, of course. This would be an unavoidable event that was preordained by you and your guides prior to the lifetime. It can be hard to accept that you planned this tragic loss, or some other traumatizing event, but you did, and you did it to learn.

Not all preordained experiences are tough and unpleasant. Meeting your soul mate and initiating a satisfying relationship can be a preordained event.

When I was 10 years old my parents separated, this was a preordained event I foresaw in the spiritual dimension prior incarnation and chose to experience—I knew this was going to happen. On the day I was told that separation was taking place, a flashback occurred in my memory.

6. Incarnation Characteristics

Traits of a life form you inherit. When you are born into the world as a male, for example, you will naturally inherit male characteristics, as they are part of the species in which you chose to incarnate. Traits for a male human may or may not include: desire to mate with the opposite sex, provide for your family, be competitive at sports, etc. When you pass from the Earth, the inherited traits of the species you are will remain here in the living dimension. The spirit will take back to the heavenly dimension all the emotional and life experiences associated with universal learning from the lifetime. So the law of incarnation characteristics gave you these gender traits of character that you have, for the most part. However, you do carry forth to future lifetime's emotional traits which you have learned or unlearned in your journey of universal learning.

7. Protection

Protection in the spiritual dimension is constant as it is your natural dimension. You will be protected from all. The saying, "under God's protection," is most true when you are in your natural dimension—Heaven.

When you leave the heavenly dimension for the living dimension, you are in the unprotected realms. As you incarnate into human life, you are on your own; with the exception of God's angels and guides—if you will open your mind to them and listen. You can pray for God's light, love, and protection, and you shall receive it, but remember; you are on the living dimensional and not in the sanctuary of Heaven.

So, while participating in a lifetime of universal learning you are essentially out on your own.

8. Time

There is no time in the spiritual universe; only in the living universe do we record time, because our physical life forms cannot last indefinitely. The living dimensions expand, grow, contract, and cease to exist, then are reborn again, therefore it is logical to have some sense of recorded time. We all find it a little strange at first to grasp this concept, but it is so. There is no measurement of time in the spiritual dimension—not a single second. So when we say you can have as many lifetimes as you need to learn "patience" (for example), then take note that it can take hundreds, if not thousands, of Earth-time years to complete.

9. Guidance

The guides are with you—24/7. Your spiritual guides are with you every second of your physical existence on Earth. The guides are here to guide and protect you, mostly on a sub-conscious level. They will only intervene on a divine scale when your life is threatened, before it is your preordained time to naturally leave the Earth dimension.

The Guides communicate with you through dreams, intuition, and feelings. You can sometimes connect with them better during prayer and meditation. The law of guidance also applies to your own higher mind which can guide your decision making process on a conscious and subconscious level.

10. Learning

Learning is indefinite—it never ends! Universal learning is a constant process. Your spiritual existence is to learn and grow. When you experience a lesson and learn it, be advised that this is subject to revocation. For example, just because you learned not to hate in a previous lifetime, you cannot give in to hate in this one. If you do, you will have to relearn the lesson again in a future lifetime.

11. Restoration

All things in the living universe come to an end. All relationships, careers, and lifetimes will come to an end. You will pass physically from this world one day and your eternal spirit will probably return to this or another living dimension to experience another lifetime. All chaos restores to order and vice versa. All order in the living universe changes, declines, and can turn into chaos. The chaos reverts into order. Look at all the great civilizations of the world: they come and they all go.

12. Free Will

The choice is yours. The law of free will denotes that you are free to choose and manifest your own life here on Earth.

Don't look for life to hand you the prizes on a plate. Taking into account your destined preordained experiences, you have the power and free will to manifest a great life, or to manifest nothing. You are free to create the life you want.

Chapter 3

What you are

Let us briefly discuss these related subjects in order to answer what you are:

- God
- Spirit
- Soul
- Higher Mind
- Heaven
- Angels & Guides

God (superior spirit)

Let us start by discussing superior spirit—God. I view God from a monotheistic perspective—that there is only one God; the superior being, the creator of all spirits, this universe, and all life forms in it.

Many people believe in a God that created the earth in a small number of days. I am not going to debate biblical beliefs or any other religious statements in this book. The information I present is based on my interpretation of the guidance that I receive from my spiritual guides. We all know the earth is over 4 billion years old. The time transformation from a sphere of hot gas to present day conditions is actually irrelevant. You may think it is relevant that something took 4 billion years to come into existence, but there is no time in the spiritual universe, therefore the formations of galaxies and living dimensions can take as long as needed. The amount of time it takes to create a universe is irrelevant. What is relevant is that the Big Bang or something else created this living dimension. Events of cosmic proportions were, and are, caused by a higher being—God. This cosmic event resulted in the formation of planet Earth and a few million others. Therefore, to say that God created the Earth is true.

God emanates unconditional love, kindness, compassion, and forgiveness for all his spirits (I will refer to God as a He for familiarity, with due respect given to the feminine). You are forgiven for every wrongdoing you commit in a lifetime, but you will redeem yourself by incarnating and learning through another lifetime. God is to be respected, but not feared, as certain worldly organizations would have you believe. The only being you need to fear is yourself, as you are the cause and effect of most of the events in your life, and not God, as you will learn through the **Universal Law of Action & Effect**. As a creation of God, you are loved and cared for on a transcendent scale—beyond the experience of the human mind. However, God's spirits will learn his ways; hence the lifetimes you undertake to grow to be like God through universal learning.

- It has been stated: **Man was created in His image**.
- Let me reword this slightly: **Man will become more in His image**.

This means you have to become more like your God, and you will. God is perfect: it is as simple as that. We have to undertake lifetimes to learn and grow to be more as He is, but we will never be Gods, so get that straight. I am sure it is difficult to comprehend how one entity can be over everything. God is not a CEO or a bullish dictator, but more like an eternal grandfather sitting on the porch, watching his children play and letting them learn by themselves.

God is worshipped in many different forms of religions. You can view God in any form you desire, or even choose to not view God at all. I wish to clearly state that human beings in general have the universal right to affiliate their faith, or no faith, in whatever form they desire. I do not subscribe at all to the view that a single religion's God, or the ways in which they worship Him, is better than another's; this attitude is nothing but bigotry. Most of the world's religions and beliefs source back, in one way or another, to the single creator of all. Therefore, most of us believe in a single, superior entity. We, the people of this Earth, need to be more understanding and tolerant on matters such as religion and beliefs. This intolerance of one another's religions and beliefs is probably the most serious problem humanity has faced since recorded time began.

I would estimate that at least 90% of all human beings sense in their minds that there is a higher power to which we all belong. Many of us are taught religion at a young age and take relatively warmly to the idea, as we seem to have more spiritual awareness about who we are in our younger years. However, as we grow older and reach our early teens, many of us become so engrossed and focused on life that we tend to put this spiritual connection into the back of our minds. This condition is normal and I was no exception, but I never once lost my belief in God and a higher power. Take note, if you were permanently aware of God and the universe and you knew it all, there would be no point in being on His Earth to experience growth.

God seems to get the blame for many things that happen in our world. On one hand, He gets praised; on the other hand, He gets criticized, and all too often, He is discarded. We need to discuss this further in order for you to understand the relationship between God and the people of planet Earth.

- Do not blame God for war and conflict. God does not make, nor desire, wars over religion; which are supposed to preach qualities such as love, forgiveness, respect, and understanding, in the first place! Those people who kill in the name of God or religion are false. Those who use religion, or any other form of belief, as justification to cause harm to others will answer for their actions and will be subject to the pain and suffering they caused to others through incarnating in future lifetimes and experiencing an equivalent level of pain and suffering as per the **Universal Law of Karma**.

- Do not blame God for earthly catastrophic events that have occurred in human history. You are currently residing on a living, breathing planet, not a perfect sanctuary.

- Do not praise God when things are going great in life, such as happy family life and a healthy financial situation, and then, when an unforeseen tragedy occurs, blame Him. Human beings are responsible for their own lives: and this is a rule you must learn for your own benefit. Too often, people praise God when they're making excellent money and feeling spiritually healthy and then when the going gets a little tough, God is not mentioned.

Human beings create their own destiny in their own lives and have always created the reality of life on Earth through their actions. An example of this: **Universal Law of Action & Effect**—every action you undertake has an effect.

- You get drunk and drive your car although you know you are over the legal alcohol limit. You know you are taking a risk by drinking and driving. You get pulled over by the police and arrested for driving while intoxicated (DWI) and receive the legal punishment as a result of the actions you undertook. You lose your job and your income, and ultimately you lose your home. You created this situation yourself; no one else did, so don't blame God.

Some people claim God does not protect them. **The Universal Law of Protection**—which we all must clearly understand--is that when we are in the spiritual dimensions, nothing but nothing can harm us. Now, here in the living dimension, we are outside of our natural environment and subject to the laws of living. Therefore, when people say God does not protect us, they are incorrect. He does so in the heavens, but on this living dimensional plain, He will not, because we have to live by the ***Universal Law of Action & Effect***.

God does not directly control events that occur on this planet; human beings do. God set the stage and gave you a pass to experience a lifetime of learning on Earth, so be thankful for that. Remember, you chose to incarnate on planet Earth and to learn and experience.

Spirit

This is who you are and will always be for all eternity. You may think of yourself as a physical human mortal, but you are purely energy residing in a physical body. Your body in this lifetime is your vehicle for experiencing life on Earth. When the time of passing occurs on Earth, the spirit departs the living dimension and returns to its heavenly dimension. You retain the memories of the life departed and all the learning experiences associated with that lifetime.

A spirit consists of a soul and a higher mind, which are inseparable, as they are the same. The spirit is neither male nor female: this concept can take a little getting used to, but it is so. Try to not compare the universe and spirituality to only your knowledge of Earth life: who is to say that there are not life forms in the Milky Way galaxy that have three or four different types of sexual orientation? We all are composed of the same energy, albeit at different stages of growth and development. Spiritual growth for a human being is to truly learn emotional and life experiences. The essence of your spiritual existence is to learn and grow. Your spirit is eternal and will never cease to exist.

Soul

I would think of the soul as the heart of the spirit. You cannot separate the soul from the higher mind, as they are part of your spiritual energy field. Many of us are used to hearing the word "soul" more than we are the word "spirit." If you choose to keep on referring to your spirit as your soul, there is no harm done. Do whatever makes you feel comfortable. When we hear the word "soul," it tends to trigger the thought in our higher minds that something dwells deeply within us. Your higher mind is telling you that your soul is part of your spirit

Your soul acts as a sponge, absorbing all of the emotions and life experiences that you have in your lifetime in the living dimensions, and your natural existence in the spiritual universe. Your higher mind records these emotional events as well, but the soul stores the emotional energy associated with the experience. You may have a strange fondness for a foreign land that you have never visited in this lifetime, and wonder where this strange fondness comes from. This fondness or attraction may come from your remembrance of a past lifetime and the emotions associated with that lifetime, and those feelings are actually comments from your soul.

Higher Mind

This is the brain of your spirit, but it is not a physical mass, such as is the human brain. Higher mind contains all the universal knowledge about who you are and what you have learned and experienced as a spirit of the universe. The higher mind stores the memories and universal spiritual logic associated with emotional and life experiences. You cannot separate the soul and its higher mind, as they are part of the same energy field of the spirit. The higher mind is also your connection to guidance and counsel from your spiritual guides during your lifetime on Earth.

Your higher mind contains knowledge and information on a universal scale.

Imagine the world's most powerful computer; you are impressed by its memory, speed, and many applications. Your higher mind is superior to the all of world's finest computers combined. In fact, you cannot compare your higher mind to any piece of man-made equipment. Your higher mind contains such a vast amount of knowledge that if you had total and unrestricted access to it for 10 seconds, you would be dumb struck; and if you were paid $1 million never to tell another human being what you had witnessed, you would forfeit the money, as you would be unable to contain yourself—and nobody would blame you.

You are able, from time to time during your lifetime on Earth, to access this universal knowledge through your higher mind, but only if it is beneficial to your goals, lessons, and purpose of your lifetime on Earth. You may think it's unfair that we have this knowledge locked inside of us and cannot access it on a permanent basis. You may wonder why this is so. Be advised that if you knew all the answers and had access to all universal knowledge, there would be no point in experiencing this lifetime.

At first, it can be rather difficult to consciously access your higher mind. This can be done through mediation, prayer, and through opening your mind to new possibilities. You will know when you have achieved this new level of awareness when the time comes.

Heaven

The spiritual dimension, "Heaven" or "the Afterworld," as it is sometimes referred to, is not of this living dimension. Your spiritual dimension, or as you more commonly know, Heaven, is your true home, as it is where you were created and belong. You travel from your heavenly spiritual dimension to this and other living dimensions to experience the lessons of universal learning and growth in each lifetime.

Heaven and the rest of the universe are made from energy, as we are, and take many visual forms. All dimensions of Heaven are interconnected and the source to the heavenly father--God. It is peace and love in its purest form and is untainted and threatened by nothing. As it is such a peaceful place, you cannot experience most emotional and situational lessons on this plane—you have to incarnate into the living dimensions to engage in learning experiences. However, some levels of learning are attained in the spiritual universe only.

All human beings at the time of passing return to their heavenly dimension—all of us, no matter what we have done or have not done. Heaven is where you will re-unite with other spirits that you have bonded with in this and other lifetimes. These other spirits are commonly referred to as "soul mates." There are an infinite number of spiritual dimensions and you do share these dimensions with your soulmates. When a human being passes from Earth, we grieve and feel a sense of loss. However, we sense that we will see them again--not quite in the same physical form—but it will be them.

Time is non-existent in Heaven, as this dimension is part of the spiritual universe; therefore, not a single second of time passes as per the ***Universal Law of Time***. We only record time in lifetimes in the living dimensions, as our physical forms that we incarnate into cannot last indefinitely.

Angels & Guides

Angels are normal spirits, as we are, but they are here with us on Earth to protect and guide us: hence the term "Guardian Angel." I refer to angels as guides.

The ***Universal Law of Guidance*** states that guides are with us from the moment we are born to protect and guide us in all aspects of life. When we pass from this world we choose either to remain on our spiritual dimension or to become guides for other spirits. As you grow in your lifetime, some guides may be replaced by others, but this is normal.

Your guides are here to help you in your lifetime. They radiate pure, unconditional love and guidance for you, no matter what you have done, not done, or will do. It is hard to imagine that someone loves you no matter what—is it not? When you seek help in your life, the guides offer counsel for you in the form of dreams, visions, intuition, and plain gut feelings on numerous issues. You may not have an instant subconscious conversation with them, as the answers may seem to take a while, and worse still, you may not like the answer! However, you will feel their presence and guidance when it is necessary in your life. The decisions are always yours to make and you must make them on your own. Remember, you are the cause and effect of your life and the decisions are yours to make.

You can learn to receive the guidance through prayer, meditation, and most of all, by having an open mind. Do you ever think of an idea or a subject and get goosebumps, feel the hair on your neck stand up, or have an overwhelmingly strong feeling about an issue? This is your guides contacting you!

There should be no fear about seeking guidance on your own or through a good psychic counselor. The guides are here to help you achieve your lessons in life and to help you in all aspects of your life. The guides will only tell you what you need to know at certain times in your life. Seek as much guidance from your spiritual guides as you see fit.

Your guides are your guardian angels and they will guide you all the way, if you listen to them. A person may say, "God guided them" to make the good decisions in their life, but it is their guides that God created to do it for them; as God created all of us, the saying "God guided me" is true from a universal perspective. If you still choose to say, "God guided me and no other," then that is fine too.

The guides will not interfere in your life, except when you face a life-threatening situation and it is not your destined time to leave the Earth dimension.

What you are is a form of eternal energy, more commonly known as a spirit. Your spirit contains your soul and your higher mind, which are inseparable. You were created by God—the superior spirit—and you are currently on planet Earth to experience a lifetime of universal learning for the growth and development of your spirit. When you pass from this Earth, you return to the heavenly dimensions where you were created and belong.

Chapter 4

Universal Learning: Why does the Spirit need to learn & grow?

Universal Learning is the journey of growth and development to become more like God. This growth and development is referred to as lessons. A lesson for a human being is to learn emotional and life experiences.

Your spirit needs to experience emotional and situational events on Earth, as well as other universal learning, in order to grow. You need to grow to become more like the creator—like God. You choose to incarnate as a human being on Earth to learn and grow.

You may ask the questions, "Why do I need to experience these emotional and situational events?" and, "I like who I am, so what's wrong with me?" For starters, there is nothing wrong with you. As a creation of universal energy, it is your purpose as a spirit to seek out and learn the ways of the universe. This universal learning is organized by one entity—God. As the spiritual and living dimensions are infinite in number, there is much to learn of the ways. For humans, learning the ways of the universe almost seems impossible to comprehend. For right now, all you need to know is that your current lifetime on Earth is part of learning the ways of the universe. Accept the knowledge that you desired to be here and you have chosen a lifetime with specific experiences for the benefit and development of your spirit. Some of your experiences may seem good or bad right now, but ultimately all experiences will benefit you in terms of growth.

Emotions known to us living on this Earth must be experienced and controlled while completing life experiences. We talk more in detail of emotional and life experiences in chapter 6. Most of the lessons we undertake will have an emotional impact on us, as we humans, and most other life forms on Earth, live and thrive off our emotional energy. We can all claim to be logical and in complete control of all situations, but ultimately all feelings and actions are governed by emotions. Control your emotions and allow them to bring you success and fulfillment in your lifetime; but as we know, this is a lot easier said than done.

Spiritual growth is achieved when the lesson is learned while observing the universal laws. You cannot merely live through the experience just to get it over with; it doesn't work like that. You must truly embrace the experience and learn from it, whether it appears to be good or bad for you at the time. Many of the lessons and experiences we choose to undertake in our lifetimes are not easy to live through.

You may ask the question, "How many lessons must I learn to deal with before I am finished?" I will answer the latter part of the question first—you are never finished! The **Universal Law of Learning** states that you will never stop learning and experiencing. Some of you might be feeling, "Oh dear, it is going to take forever to learn all these lessons and we are never going to be finished." This is because there is no finish line! Remember, there is no time in the spiritual universe, none whatsoever— the **Universal Law of Time**. It is rather difficult to comprehend this, but it is so. With that understanding, it appears we do have plenty of time— an eternity's worth! In respect to never being finished; have you ever seen a poster that states: "The race for quality has no finish line?" My analogy is that the evolution of the spirit is a quality development program too. Hopefully you see the comparison now.

When you have completed your learning on Earth, you will move on to new levels of learning and experiencing in the physical and spiritual universe. This will be the next level of learning for you. Upon attaining this level, you will be an advanced Earth spirit. However, that is not to say that an advanced spirit is not permitted back on Earth. Many advanced spirits are here now in physical form to assist other spirits in life and to help our struggling world in all matters.

The essence of the spirit is to learn and grow: that is the purpose of your universal existence, and that is why you are here on Earth right now.

Some of you now might say, in a hypothetical conversation with me:

"Oh, this is becoming too much now, and so much to learn, and to top it all, we never really get finished universally neither. Forget it man!"

Really! That is why you love coming back to Earth to learn, is it not?

"No, that is not true. I do not like my life, and besides, I have no clue about the meaning of life!"

So, why did you come back to the living dimension then?

Now you struggle to find a reply, don't you? In your higher mind, you know the above has some sense of universal truth.

Currently we are incarnated onto the living dimension, which is subject to the laws of physics, time, etc. Our human brain finds it difficult to relate to the concept of universal learning, in respect to dimensions where there is no start, no end, and even no time. How can you survive without a watch! Try and relate universal teachings to outside the normal Earth living-thinking pattern. This abstract thinking takes a little time to get accustomed to, but things will make more sense to you the more you open your mind to it. Look out to the clear night sky, relax, and open your mind and reflect for a moment on what you have just read.

Human beings seem to experience the most on Earth, and that is why so many spirits want to return to the living dimensions, in the living universe, as a general type of humanoid. People on Earth, we call humans, and those not from this world, we call extraterrestrials. There are many forms of living humanoids and other life forms in the living universe—many of them.

I feel as though I have learned over the ages of time on this particular dimension. My desire to open my mind and learn universal teachings, at times, is almost uncontrollable—in a positive sense. I desire to learn and grow as a spirit should, and it feels good and natural to me.

Part 1

Chapter Summary Points

- Universe: The Universe consists of infinite spiritual and living dimensions that are transcendent in scale. The spiritual dimensions are places like the heavens and other realms. An example of a living dimension is the Milky Way galaxy.

- Energy: The infinite universe and all of its contents, whether living or spiritual dimensions, are classified as forms of energy—all of it. That means our homes, cars, human bodies; heaven, your spirit, your thoughts, and even God are forms of energy.

- Universal Laws: These are a set of rules that guide our universal existence, which include both the spiritual and living dimensions.

- What you are: A form of eternal energy, more commonly known as a spirit. Your spirit contains your soul and your higher mind, which are inseparable. You were created by God—the superior spirit.

- Universal Learning: The journey of growth and development to become more like God.

Part 2

The Lifetime—Why you are here on Earth

Now that you have an understanding of "Who you are," you may ask the questions now: "Why am I here and what is the meaning of life?" These questions must be asked at least 5,000 times a day by humans on planet Earth.

In Part Two, we shall discuss the lifetime, and then move on to emotional and life experiences. We will progress to the path and the choices you will face in your lifetime. The natural ending and previous lifetimes will conclude Part Two.

Chapter 5

Lifetime

This is the meaning of your life: You are here on Earth with the objective to learn and understand God's ways through universal learning. You will undertake this universal learning by experiencing lessons for spiritual growth. A lesson for a spirit incarnated as a human being on Earth is to learn emotional and life experiences. This learning is your purpose in life. You engage in universal learning because it is the essence of your existence to learn the ways of the universe, and because of your love for the superior spirit: the *Universal Law of Learning.*

This lifetime is a precious gift from God--the superior spirit. A lifetime is a chance to experience, learn, and develop your spirit by incarnating into a life form: in this case a human being in the Milky Way galaxy living dimension.

This is how a lifetime starts:

- While in your heavenly spiritual dimension prior to incarnation, you decide and plan--in consultation with other soulmates, spirits, guides, and not forgetting God-- what is to be the next step in your development of universal learning and which living dimension to pursue this in. Remember, there are an infinite number of living dimensions and universal learning is infinite by its nature; therefore, each living and spiritual dimension offers different universal learning experiences.

- In your consultation, you may all decide that emotions, such as jealousy and aggressiveness, have been experienced, but not truly learned and controlled. Therefore, you all decide how best to experience these lessons again, and this will be your destiny. You all agree on incarnation as a human being on Earth. You decide who will be your parents, the likely upbringing, and the social environment. You will also format your traits and talents for your lifetime. Every human being is good at one thing at least; either in sports, arts, commerce, or whatever. Also, who will incarnate with you as soulmates and who will be the guides. Bear in mind that guides can change as needed during a lifetime.

- During this pre-life consultation, you will have visions and glimpses of your life prior to birth: such as people, places, and life situations that you will encounter. Most of you have experienced Déjà vu at one point in your life. Where does this come from? It comes from the visions and glimpses prior to your lifetime, which are stored in your higher mind. Déjà vu can also be from dreams of foretelling by your guides that you have with you in this current lifetime.

- The transition from the spiritual, heavenly dimension to the human body is effortless. Although it seems a little confined at first, we all get use to it and then settle down to our lifetime on Earth.

Your existence on this world is subject to **twelve universal laws**. All the universal laws are equally important; however, a few of these laws warrant more discussion in their relation to a lifetime, as they are fundamental and will have a predominant effect on your chosen lifetime and the course that it will follow.

- The ***Universal Law of Preordination*** states that we all have a destiny. That is, certain experiences in our life are preordained; meaning that certain events may happen in your life that are destined to take place. We all learn lessons in life that at the time seem very hard on us, and it can be tough to accept these. However, when you realize and identify with your current lifetime, these tough experiences seem to make more sense to you.

- Now, while some experiences are preordained, other events and experiences are open; meaning you will have to work to attain them. You will not become the fruit farmer, accountant, or the highly skilled artist that you were destined to be if you are not prepared to work for it: As the ***Universal Law of Action and Effect*** dictates: no work, no reward.

- Although you have a destiny through preordination, there is nothing that can prevent you from having a better, more exciting life than what was planned by you and your guides. You always have the power to change and better yourself. The saying, "Be all you can be," is most true. Remember you have free will as per the ***Universal Law of Free Will***.

- You may have to redeem yourself in this lifetime for your actions in a past lifetime. You may have committed a criminal act and wish to redeem yourself. Your desire for redemption stems from your love of God. If you do not want to redeem your spirit, then you will be sent into a lifetime of redemption for your spirit. This is done for your own growth, and it is the ***Law of Karma:*** you get out what you put in. The universal laws will always be honored one way or another. We all make mistakes and errors in judgment so don't worry if you are coming to the realization that you have made some poor choices in this lifetime, or even in past ones.

- The **Universal Law of Incarnation**—inheriting characteristics of your chosen life form. As we have ascertained, a spirit is neither male nor female in its form in the spiritual dimension. When you incarnate into a male or female body, you will assume most of the emotional and physiological characteristics associated with that species. Most men seem to have natural desire to be competitive and defend their home and family; and most women seem to have a natural desire to give birth to children and nurture them. Do not be too concerned if you have neither of the aforementioned traits, as we all cannot be the same. Depending on your chosen human form, you will assume these and additional characteristics. You will also have with you traits from previous lifetimes—this is part of the **Universal Law of Karma**. Remember, it is the lessons from the experiences in life that your spirit will absorb and learn. When your life physically ends, you will return to the spiritual dimensions with all the universal learning experiences from your lifetime.

Most of all the human beings born into the world are here for universal learning, however, there are spirits who are born to help others learn and to aid this planet Earth. These spirits have critical, preordained roles to fulfill and many of the religious master teachers that have come to Earth are examples of this. Also, certain spirits are here mainly to live and experience life again. For example, let's assume you desire another lifetime of marriage with a soul mate to share love and happiness just for the thrill of it, or you desire another lifetime as a master craftsman. This can be so with God's blessing. Life is a most precious gift, I tell you. Have you ever heard the comment "bliss on tap?"

Well, God can give you bliss any time you want. The only thing you have to do is prove yourself. Ask Him for it, and you shall receive.

When discussing lifetimes, many people talk of destiny, marrying soul mates, and so on. As events unfold in your life, there is a possibility, however small, that you miss out on some of your preordained events through your own extreme actions, or extraordinary events beyond your control. You may be concerned that your life will now become meaningless and empty. This may initially be the case as you adjust to find a new path to follow. Your guides will help you shape a new destiny with new goals of universal learning for you.

There is a debate in New Age circles as to whether certain events in the world's history were preordained for our benefit.

Meaning certain spirits volunteered to live a lifetime for the benefit of others, whether in be good or bad; recent events in world history, such as World War II and the Holocaust, for example—were these events meant to be or not? People like Hitler, Stalin, Churchill, and Roosevelt; did they come here to start and end these events for the benefit of spiritual experience and growth? I personally think the likes of Hitler and Stalin were evil, and Churchill and Roosevelt were guided to defend the righteous against tyranny. I do think hijacking nations and perverting their laws, persecution, mass murder, and wars based on racial purity and ideology are not needed for our spiritual development at all. You can experience struggle and hardship in your average life without destroying millions of innocent life forms and damaging the environment of planet Earth.

Every human being has a right to basic freedom, with fair laws, in whatever country or territory they reside in. Human beings also need to realize that they are subject to these territorial laws during their lifetime. For instance, if you commit murder unjustifiably, then you will be punished accordingly. Be advised though, that receiving and completing a judicial punishment does not get you off the hook, as far as the universal laws are concerned. **A human being should never suffer under the tyranny of oppression or brutality of any state, or by any one person. A lifetime is not meant for the total oppression of the spirit.** The universe, meaning the guides, will never sit back and do nothing about evil orchestrated events, but as I said earlier, don't blame God or the universe for our situations on this Earth, as we control the fate of this world. Human beings have to make a better place for all, and we must do it ourselves.

You have to realize that in the living universe, your lifetimes are not perfect, loving, peaceful, and full of bliss 24/7. All of these qualities are of the heavenly spiritual dimensions. However, you must make your lifetime as loving, peaceful, and fulfilling as possible, and you can.

Have you ever dreamed about being in the movies or television, living out the parts of different heroes and wishing that you had a life with such variety? Well, you do, even better than that because your existence as a spirit gives you access to all the lifetimes of universal experiencing, and the part that you play in each lifetime is real— very real indeed!

I believe in my life, here and now, that I chose to undertake the following lessons:

- Controlling my emotions (extremely hard when losing golf balls off the tee box)
- Forgiveness and forgetting the past
- Sacrificial love
- Staying to life's path no matter what
- Achieving a good balance in life
- Writing and teaching New Age philosophy

There will no doubt be a few more preordained events that will present themselves in my life to challenge me— no doubt!

Chapter 6

Emotional & Life Experiences

Now that we understand where we are from, and the concept of a lifetime of universal learning, we ask the question: "What exactly is it we have to learn from this dimension that Earth is a part of?"

We have to learn the emotional and life experiences that Earth living can offer, such as love, fear, integrity, and hardship, to name a few. The lessons we undertake by experience must truly be learned, controlled, and in some cases, overcome, such as the weakness of addiction to drugs, alcohol, and even food. We design our lifetimes on Earth around universal learning and these experiences are the meaning of your life.

Most emotional and life experiences are interrelated. There are many of these interrelated experiences to learn from, so it will take many lifetimes to truly master them: some might take a few attempts -- trust me on this.

In life, we have many experiences and face many issues. But the question is; how many do we truly learn? Remember that although you learn a lesson in this life, you may abuse the experience and break the *Universal Law of Learning* in future lifetimes and have to relearn it again.

There are positive and negative emotions and life experiences, some are pleasant and others are not so pleasant. We say this, in not a judicial sense that you are scowled upon if you make errors in judgment concerning negative emotions and experiences. Please understand, it all comes to down to one thing: learning. You are here to learn and you will make mistakes. We all do. You must truly learn from your mistakes and be prepared to repay karmic debts. Please be advised that not every single emotion and experience that it is relative to this living dimension is listed here in this book.

First, we will list some of the main emotions known to us as humans on Earth. These will be some of our emotional lessons that we may face in this and multiple lifetimes.

Positive Emotions

Love—the main emotion we all relate to is love. The emotion of love encompasses much and can have different effects on people of different cultures and background. In love, we have a deep and tender feeling for a person or thing.

We will learn to love each other, life, God, and ourselves. We experience love in every lifetime as love for our parents or guardians, family, friends, etc. Love is the most common emotion we feel in our daily lives. Love is the cornerstone of our spiritual existence. As the strongest emotion, the saying, "Love conquers all," is most true.

You must love yourself in your life. People may think this is a selfish concept; however, you are no good to anyone if you do not love yourself first. You will be negative and unattractive to people if you do not love yourself.

I would say that forgiveness of another is drawn from love, because it is through the power of love that forgiveness is achieved.

Unconditional Love—love that is unbreakable, undiminished by anything. Is true love unconditional love? Well, we could debate that back and forth, but let us look at two examples:

- You will still love your brother even though he steals money from you to buy alcohol, as he is suffering from an addiction problem. You can confront him and address the situation as you deem appropriate, but your love should not diminish.

- Your grown-up child informs you that he is a homosexual now. This can be a bit of a shock for some parents, but their love for their child should not be affected, as their grown-up child's personal and private life is his business and not really his parent's.

Compassion—the feelings of sympathy or pity for the sufferings of another along with a natural urge to help them, for example:

- You exhibit compassion by assisting another suffering person, or even an organization, in whatever way you can; perhaps, contributing to a world charity or donating some of your possessions to a single parent household.

To show empathy is a form of compassion. It is always good to put yourself in someone else's shoes before you make judgment. Forgiveness works very closely with compassion.

Fulfillment—to realize and achieve your conscious and subconscious goals, and ambitions. When you are fulfilled, you feel happy and content. For example:

- You may feel this emotion in a marriage or friendship, or even in your career. Prior to your lifetime, you will have pre-determined goals of universal learning, of which you are only aware at a subconscious level for the most part. When you realize these goals, you will experience a great inner sense of fulfillment.

To be fulfilled on a permanent basis would be a state of absolute bliss. Fulfillment is one of the happiest and most satisfying states of mind that you can achieve in any living dimension.

Contentment—being content is at a state of calmness. It is being happy with what you have or achieve, and not desiring something more or different. Only you will know when you are content. Many of us find this contentment when we marry and settle down, for example.

- Retirement is a state in which many people feel contentment in their lives. When you realize and fulfill personal goals, you feel a sense of contentment, and rightly so.

Contentment is a very satisfying emotion to feel, as it brings a sense of calmness to your spirit. Fulfillment can bring a sense of contentment into one's life.

Happiness—a feeling of great joy and gladness.

Many people will feel happiness if their baseball team has just won the World Series; others, by meeting their partner in life, or by winning the lottery.

I tend to view happiness as being loved, fulfilled, and content. If a person can realize the aforementioned emotions, then they truly must be happy.

Negative Emotions

Fear—having a sense of anxiety, apprehension, or dread about a person, event, or thing. Fear is a crippling emotion, as it affects our lives and nullifies growth. Let us say for example:

- That you have a chronic fear of flying and you cannot go to a Career Development conference in New York that you wish to attend. The emotion of fear has dominated the event for career growth and affected your life.

When we have chronic fears, we often seek guidance, and rightly so. Do not be afraid to seek out those who can help you overcome your fears. There are some things in life that you have a human right to be frightened about, such as your house burning down or losing a loved one. Fear, as all negative emotions, is a part of the spirit and you must learn to control it and not let it dominate your lifetime of learning.

Anger—when emotional control is lost and displeasure at a person or thing occupies your higher mind and all clear logical thinking is obstructed by this state, for example:

- You can get angry when driving your car and almost have an accident due to someone carelessly driving and almost causing you to crash your vehicle.

- You can feel anger towards your partner during, and even after, a disagreement.

- You can get angry when you don't get your own way and things don't go as planned in life.

Anger is a dangerous emotion and you must be careful with it, because if you cannot control your anger it will cause you to act irrationally and do harm to yourself and to others.

Jealousy—being in a resentful state over a person's possession, achievements, or their relationships, for example:

- You can be jealous over a friend dating a girlfriend or boyfriend whom you desire.

- You can be jealous over a peer who received a promotion for a job.

- You also can be jealous of people in general life, because you are submerged in negative emotions and you cannot better your own life, and therefore resent others and are ultimately jealous of them.

Hate—the state where you totally dislike and vent negative thought energy to a person or idea. An example of hate:

- When a person's partner commits an adulterous act and you hate them for what they did to your relationship.

- Or your boss dismisses you unfairly and you cannot receive legal compensation.

- You can also hate an ethnic or certain classification of people or things.

Hate is not a good state of affairs and it should be avoided at all costs. Hate is total negative energy and will breed total negative results. You can and are allowed to dislike a person or thing, but accept them for what they did or are, and move on with your own life.

Revenge—the desire to strike back or get even with someone whom you perceive as having done you harm, for example:

- You may desire revenge over a partner's unfaithful act, your boss' wrongful dismissal, or because a work colleague stole your idea and received credit for it. These are all examples that can stimulate and manifest the act of revenge.

By committing the same wrongful act, you would be no better than the person who committed the first offense.

While we list emotions as positive and negative, we say it is all experiencing and learning. Please be advised though that succumbing to negative emotions will only bring you a lifetime of discontentment, non-fulfillment, and suffering.

Life Experiences

Secondly, we can list some of the life experiences we choose to undertake and face. As I said, many of these you may classify as emotional, but the overriding factor is that they have to be experienced and learned, irrespective of where we think they belong:

Marriage—to share a lifetime of commitment to a partner. Marriage is a common life experience, which is experienced in numerous lifetimes. Most marry a member of the opposite sex; some people have civil unions or partnership agreements with members of the same sex, but the experience of commitment to a partner remains.

Motherhood—to give birth and raise children. Some of you may think this has to be done for the human race to survive—you are correct. Most spirits of the universe will gladly reincarnate to mother their soul mates and spirits of God, to assist them in their lifetime of learning. Some spirits simply live for the benefit for other spirits to live and learn.

As I was born into this world as a male, the thought of giving birth nearly makes me violently ill and faint. This is a normal reaction as I am physically subject to the *Universal Law of Incarnation* and I inherited male characteristics, thus, childbirth is not on the checklist—period, no debate!

Adherence to the Life Path—to stick to your destiny and goals in life no matter how tough it gets. This can be a very difficult lesson to learn, believe me. You will know as time passes, whether you have achieved this. Adhering to your life path involves tapping into your knowledge of patience, commitment, hard work, and inner guidance.

There are so many things that test us along the pathway of life. The experience of a staying on your chosen life path involves a lot of hard work and commitment.

Faithfulness—to not commit an unfaithful act in a committed relationship and/or to be unloyal in some other earthy cause. This is one of those experiences that most human beings struggle with. If we don't actually commit the act, we actually drive ourselves nearer to it by activating our thoughts towards it. Your thoughts can really become your reality. As you create the energy associated with the desire, your thought energy will drive those desires towards manifestation—so be careful what you think, as you may get it.

Forgiveness—to learn to forgive and move on after a hurtful act has been committed against you. Tough experience to learn, but we face this in every lifetime. Somebody always hurts you very badly on an emotional level, or to a lesser degree, on a physical level. Look at it his way, if only one person or thing hurts you, count yourself lucky.

Your ability to forgive is drawn from the power of love. By observing the ***Universal Law of Emotional Control*** you will be able to forgive over time. When you loose control of this law and veer off into the hate and revenge emotions, life gets ugly.

I am a firm believer in standing your ground on issues you believe in, and always physically defending yourself. However, when the smoke clears and the calm of day returns, just remember the lesson you learned from it and move on.

Guilt—you will learn to let go of your guilt and acknowledge the life lesson. You did what you did, and what is done is done, whether it is past lifetimes or this one. Learn from judgment calls, it is all learning. You will not be lined up in heaven and shot, or cast into a fire--that's fairly tale rubbish.

Learn from what you did, forgive yourself, and move on to positive things in your life. You can still make amends in this lifetime for your lesser actions.

Sex—to experience sexual activities and the related associated passions. This is a common characteristic of life as a human being. Most of us participate in sexual activity with members of the opposite, or even the same gender. Like marriage, this experience can be repeated numerous times. Sex is more of a characteristic of a human being I would say, but it still has to be experienced by a spirit. I would caution though, that sexual conduct, behavior, and addiction all have to be controlled.

Gay—to experience a lifetime of being a homosexual. You may have cruelly discriminated against gays in a previous lifetime, and so you may now experience such a treatment. There is no escaping the ***Universal Law of Karma.***

Some people who are gay choose to have civil unions or partnership agreements to experience a marriage of sorts with a member of the same sex. This is acceptable in the universe and no harm is done. It is a spirit's right to choose and live out his or her learning experiences, as long as they don't clash with the universal laws.

Honor—a feeling of doing things in a respectful, ethical, and lawful manner. This can be achieved in different ways on Earth, such as serving in the military or adhering to some other ethical code of conduct in your life. We also say that honor is the feeling of justice and righteousness. Being trustworthy can be an honorable title.

Patience—having to wait your time on things. You can be waiting on getting pregnant, desiring a new car, which you can afford, but not quite yet, and therefore you must wait. Most of us have to be patient about meeting the right type of partner in our life—hence all the bad dates and stinker relationships.

Patience can really drive a lot of people round the twist, but it's something they have to learn, as things take time to manifest.

Positive—to be positive thinking as opposed to pessimistic and negative about everything. Your thoughts can become reality. You can learn to manifest much in life through positive, realistic, and honest thinking, which will generate the necessary universal energy.

Sitting around and complaining about things will get you nowhere. Do something about it.

Commitment—to remain committed to an idea, person, or project. When the going gets tough, you have to work through the issues and stay on track. You can experience this in a marriage, project at work, or some other goal; say in a marriage when you and your partner are not seeing eye-to-eye on a few things, work at the problems and demonstrate commitment to solve them.

Integrity—to show that you posses this quality. Many people preach integrity, especially in the business field, but fall way short. Organizations advertise and claim this and claim that and in reality many their claims fall short. When you lie, cheat, make false statements, or manipulate anything, you lose your integrity. That rules out a few million people wouldn't you say? We have an eternity's worth of time, folks, so it can take as long as it needs to take.

Truthfulness—you have to be truthful. Let's say you are in the witness stand being grilled by the District Attorney who knows you witnessed a criminal act. The problem is that the act was committed by a friend. What do you do? You decide.

You must have the truth in life, as it is the only way to reach your destination. Truth is like the starting point of anything; if you don't have the truth, you have nothing to begin with.

Now, your life is your business, and all of us have the right to privacy. However, when your life is over, you may be surprised to find out that all along the truth was known to the entire spiritual universe.

Hard Work—to demonstrate that you can work hard to reach your goals. The experience is almost a prerequisite for a lifetime of learning on Earth, as you will probably get nowhere in this world if you don't work hard.

Sacrifce—you have to sacrifice one thing for another in your lifetime. Let's say you have the dream career job and all the material wealth that comes with it. However, your family life is strained because of all of the hours you work. You have to make a choice here. Which will it be?

Grief—this can be a very tough lesson as it usually involves the loss of a loved one. When we lose a loved one it can be traumatic, to say the least, and it is natural to grieve for your loss. The experience of grief is a sad one to live through, but it is almost an inherent event of life as a human being, because we all eventually will pass from Earth.

We all must learn to overcome grief in time and move on with our lives.

Tolerance—to be more understanding towards things. We can say that you can learn tolerance by acknowledging other people's political and religious views on issues.

How many times have you seen dinner parties ruined by people talking politics? Why? Don't blame the politicians (for a change) blame yourselves. If you were tolerant of other people's views and let them express themselves, then you could have an intellectually stimulating conversation instead of a hotheaded argument, which benefits no one. By listening to others, you might learn something. The same principle holds true for discussions about religion.

Intolerance and misunderstandings are crippling our world. This must not be allowed to continue. We all need to obey national and international laws and agree to work together as human beings of the universe, to create a better world to live in.

Hardship—to experience a tough lifetime or not have many resources. You can experience this by living in tough conditions in the many poor and underdeveloped areas of the world. Let me say that a person who is poor and struggling in our materialistic world should not be looked down upon. That spirit may have learned more than many others have, but chose to experience hardship, or just to live in hardship again, to confirm the experience.

Physical Imparity—physical limitations in your life. Some spirits will choose to be born with disabilities and learn to live without certain bodily functions. Those spirits that choose to incarnate in this manner seem to have more courage than most of the entire human population.

Charity—the act of giving unselfishly. This is harder when you live and reside in the materialistic areas of the world. Look at the performance that many churches go through each Sunday to get people to contribute to the church, of all places! Giving some of your hard earned assets to those who are unable to work for a living is an example of charity.

Negative Thinking—negative thought perception. You will not achieve much in life by emanating negative thoughts, as you are simply generating negative energy that will manifest itself into negative results. You have to work through this state of mind.

Greed—never being satisfied. Having a relentless desire for a thing and never being satisfied with the quantity is called greed. This state must be overcome. People can be greedy with food and money, but especially with money.

Addiction—being addicted to things. You can be addicted to alcohol, drugs, food, and other things; many people are even addicted to watching TV.

Alcohol and drug abuse are absolute killers for human beings. Excessive use of these will result in a life of addiction and ultimately, suffering. Universal learning is to experience it all and addiction is part of that too, and like all addictions, they must be overcome.

Cheating—breaking rules to achieve a goal; achieving a goal by breaking known rules. You may cheat on an academic exam to gain a qualification. This is most unsatisfactory and will be repaid in Karmic debts.

Stealing—theft, or taking what does not belong to you without permission. Stealing is taking what does not belong to you. You steal an object for your benefit. This is unacceptable behavior and will be dealt with in Karmic debts.

Lying—the opposite of being truthful. You lied in a courtroom to protect a business associate. This would be a wrong act to commit. You may set off a chain of events that were not ordained. In the end, the truth will always be known.

The opposite of the truth, lying, is a negative action. You will be deceiving yourself as well as others, and in the end, no one will gain.

Pride—the self-esteem and ego can be a good thing in terms of the quality of a person's work ethic. However, pride can be self-destructive when it clouds your logical, rational judgment in important matters. As an example, you have a disagreement with your partner and you know it was mainly your fault, but you will not apologize because your pride won't let you.

Self Pity—feeling sorry for one's self. This can leave a spirit wallowing in its own sympathy. Learn from your errors and move on. This state of mind must be overcome. It must be overcome because by engulfing yourself in pity and you will not progress in life and ultimately you'll get nowhere.

Control of Passion—mastering your temper and desires. One must be able to control their temperament. Emotional outbursts can ruin a relationship and career in an instant. Desires must be controlled, as an incident of infidelity can ruin a marriage.

Murder, Rape, Terrorism, etc.—these are not experiences to learn and are not permitted. Any spirit who kills in cold-blood, kills in the name of God, or commits criminal acts such as rape, will be subject to all the universal laws. They will be sent back here to experience the equivalent treatment that they handed out in their previous lifetimes.

This does not apply to those who kill in self-defense, or those serving in the military and acting in defense of their nation. However, you cannot commit atrocities and simply say, "I was obeying orders."

These are some of the life experiences you will face during your spiritual growth in the Earth dimension. Some of these may pleasant and some may be tough, but remember it is all only learning.

To draw an example; in my life, I have had to learn to: **Adhere to the Life Path**.

I have lived in four countries and on three different continents. I have moved my home 15 times in 23 years. I have enjoyed good career and academic success, although this has come at a high price. I have endured some tough career situations and personal sacrifices along the way. I had to work full-time and study part-time, since I left school at the age of 16 in England. Even right now, I am studying for a Business Management Degree in the USA. I think and hope I am sticking to my life path so far.

Chapter 7

The Path & Choices

As your life progresses along your chosen path, you will be faced with many choices that will have a major impact on the outcome of your life.

As we have ascertained, prior to your birth you chose this life and the experiences that you would face. You also chose how your life would evolve in order for you to engage in these learning experiences. This will become the life path for you once you incarnate into the living dimension.

People love talking about destiny, as it feels like something out of a movie or fairytale for them. You know what? They are right! In chapter 5, I mentioned that lifetimes were like movies, except that they are real—very real. Destiny is your preordained experiences that are meant to happen, such as divorce of your parents, or your marriage to a teenage sweetheart. I would say that there is always a slight chance of preordained events not happening due to extraordinary reasons. Destiny is also your open experiences, which are goals for you, which you have to work toward to achieve, such as being a doctor or a skilled artist. Therefore, your destiny is made up of preordained experiences as well as experiences that require you to put forth effort in order to achieve your goal.

You may be wondering how you are supposed to know what to choose, when, and how. Your life from birth is pretty much set up for you; the stage has been set, and all you have to do is make the choices. Your guides will lead you all the way along the path, and if you will open your heart and mind to them, your decisions will seem easier to make. You will feel which decisions are right for you when the time comes, and which decisions are only for the benefit of your selfish ego. Most of us know what is right or wrong, and what is ethical and unethical, and we really have no excuse for our conduct at times.

I will give you two different examples here of the effect that that choices can have in your life. This is about a young man named Peter. He is from a stable home environment and fairly average neighborhood.

- Peter worked hard in high school and received good grades. He had fun in school and kept himself away from trouble. He was able to go to his preferred college when he was 18. Peter, through his work ethic, also worked part-time. His family paid for part of his education, and he paid for the outstanding portion of schooling expenses. Peter graduated from college with a high GPA and now works at a financial institution. Peter now desires to be a fund manager in later years. He has just embarked on his master's degree program.

Peter, through his decisions to work hard and keep out of trouble in school, has enabled himself to land a good job and a promising career.

- Peter was a little lazy at school, and fooled around with the boys and liked to be seen as cool. He did not receive good grades and was not accepted into the college her preferred at 18. Peter had to enroll in a community college and complete two years of school prior to being accepted into his preferred college. Peter's family had warned him during his high school days that due to his lack of effort, no college funding would be available if his school grades did not pick up: they fulfilled their threat. Peter now is struggling financially. Due to this added strain and Peter's still lazy attitude at times, his GPA was not very good on completion of his degree. Peter was not selected to interview at the financial institution because of his GPA. Peter cannot embark on his master's degree because he is financially strapped and cannot acquire a good entry level job.

Peter, through his decisions **not** to work hard and keep out of trouble in school, has **not** enabled himself to land a good job and a promising career.

This was an example of the ***Universal Law of Action & Effect*** on the choice of whether to work hard and stay focused. As you can see, the end result says it all. I could give you more life and career examples, but I am sure I have gotten the point across.

During your lifetime on earth, you will be faced with many choices on your path that will determine the outcome of your life. Some of these choices may seem difficult, as you are not quite ready emotionally, spiritually, or even financially to undertake them. The wheel of fate works for everyone on Earth and if you have not, or do not make the choices and take the chances that are presented to you, and then the wheel of fate will pass along to another. Will no action on a choice be to your benefit or detriment in terms of universal learning? In your heart, you will know if you made the right choice or not. We all have to take risks in life and, sometimes, these risks can seem immense, but when the dust settles and the ship has sailed and you're still standing on the dock; what does it feel like, after the fear you let overcome you has gone, and you're left reflecting upon missed opportunities? The ***Universal Law of Action & Effect***— you took no action, and you gave into fear—the ***Universal Law of Emotional Control***.

Life will go on and new goals and all universal learning will be formatted for you to experience by your guides. However, you may have a feeling of a missed opportunity, but remember, it's all learning, so accept it and move on.

Those spirits that break the **Universal Law of Emotion Control** and give in to hate and revenge and then make the choice to commit a destructive act, will find their life paths and destiny spiraling out of control. I refer to people who commit murder, rape, willful acts of hurt, and not forgetting hate-filled acts of terrorism. Although all sins are forgiven, the **Law of Karma** will send back every ounce of pain you dish out and it will serve it on a plate for you to experience. Always physically defend yourself and respectfully state your opinions on what you believe, but think twice before you act on emotional and irrational impulses, and never deliberately hurt someone.

I want to list some scenarios, are created by your decisions that can affect your life path greatly:

- Under age drinking
- Under age tobacco use
- Under age sex
- Drug abuse
- Petty crime

You may think you are past this. You are a fully grown adult! Yes, you are, but chances are that you may have children or grandchildren, and those listed scenarios above are not good choices as they generally lead to difficult times, so let them know this.

Now, let's list a few common scenarios that are created from decisions that will negatively affect an adult's life path:

- Alcohol abuse
- Drug abuse
- Laziness
- Infidelity
- Violence
- Fraud
- Unethical business conduct

You may think, "Good grief! There is so much of this going on in the world, not to mention all the other nasty scenarios that are not even listed." As you can imagine, when you make these choices it can only lead to negative results all round.

Now, let's list decisions that will positively affect a person's life path:

- Set goals
- Work hard
- Be positive but realistic
- Be ethical
- Obey the Laws of the land
- Follow the Universal Laws
- Be loving and compassionate
- Defend yourself and your rights

You can make these decisions quite easily in your life, no matter who you are, where you are from, or where you are. You are here on Earth to learn and you can only learn by experiencing. You have to make choices in life to experience. In the previous chapter, we listed some experiences that are quite tough, and you may think it's your destiny to suffer and put up with all those negative emotions and experiences. You are not here to suffer, but you must overcome difficulties by your decisions alone, and hope that it will lead you to find success and fulfillment in your life.

The ***Universal Law of Action & Effect*** is very prominent in the life path and choices, because for every action there is a reaction. You have the power in your life to make your life better or worse. Your intentions will create your thoughts, and your thoughts will create an energy field. The energy field may manifest itself, and you will face the decisions you created. What decisions will you make to better your life?

I left school at 16, and I made the choice to work hard at Technical College, which was part of my apprenticeship training. I was fortunate enough to be entered into a nationwide competition for decorative faux painting, for which I received a commendation. As a result of this, I received trade journal and local press coverage. That same year I was awarded the "best student of the year" for my academic accomplishments. These awards, along with other credentials, enabled me to legally move overseas and to continue working and educating myself. Fourteen years later to this day in the United States all of America, I am still studying. My decision to work hard and to continually educate myself has enabled me to remain on my path in life.

Chapter 8

The Natural Ending

When our physical existence ceases on planet Earth, our spirit leaves the living dimension and returns to the heavenly spiritual dimension where it belongs. Death, whether you choose to accept it or not, is as natural as birth. It is the end of the journey of the lifetime. All physical things come to an end— the *Universal Law of Restoration.* There is nothing to fear about life after death. It is the fear of the event of passing, and how it will happen, that seems to make us a little apprehensive, and that's understandable.

For most of us, our lifetimes will end in their preordained manner. This passing could be by old age, illness, or a type of accident. However, sometimes our lives are cut short by natural events like an earthquake, flood, or an accident, such as automobile collision. These unfortunate accidents are the risks we all take by incarnating onto a living, breathing planet. Now, what is extremely unfortunate is death by murder, hate-filled terrorism (such as 9/11), and unnecessary, unjustifiable wars or conflicts.

The transformation from living to spiritual dimension is almost instantaneous. Upon departing from your body, you will sense peace and love in its purest form and you will be untainted and feel unthreatened— the *Universal Law of Protection.* When you are in your true spirit form, you will have all the knowledge and wisdom you learned during this lifetime and have access again to all the learning that you gained from your previous lifetimes. You will also have access to all of the universal knowledge stored in your higher mind. All spirits return to their heavenly dimensions, no matter what they have done on Earth. Do not despair at the end of your lifetime if you have sinned heavily, because you will return to heaven; you will redeem yourself in future incarnations.

Upon arriving at your heavenly dimension, you will be reunited with your soulmates from this lifetime and others. You will also be with spirits of the universe and your creator and mentor--God.

When people lose a loved one through natural aging or sudden loss, it is sad and to grieve is natural. You are allowed to grieve and so let it be what it is. As the days and weeks go by after a passing occurs, your life may feel empty and directionless, but this will get better with time. Take comfort in the knowledge that although your physical relationship with that spirit has ceased for now, your universal, eternal relationship is the same. That same person that you miss— and we all miss someone—is probably with you right now as you read this paragraph.

From a spiritual perspective, your loved ones will never truly leave you, and when the time comes, you will be there for those who loved you.

Chapter 9

Previous Lifetimes of Learning

Past lives are important because their energy and experiences are part of your spirit. Have you ever heard people talk about past lives or reincarnation? The reason that many people love to think about it is because, in their higher mind, they know the idea seems to bear some universal truth.

Past lifetimes are your previous lifetimes as a life form. All life forms contain an energy source which, as we discussed, is their spirit. The spirit is free to travel to any living or spiritual plane in pursuit of universal learning.

Your past lifetime may have ended five years prior to your birth in this life, or it may have ended 1,400 years ago. This may even be your first lifetime on this Earth as a human being.

Past lifetime memories are stored in your higher mind and your soul has absorbed the emotional feeling associated with events. While you are incarnated in a living dimension, the memories stored in your higher mind will generally not be readily available to you. You will sense them as feelings and intuitions on issues or situations you may have lived through and learned. When you pass from Earth, you will gain full access to your higher mind, which contains all of your memories and universal knowledge. While you are here in the living dimension engaged in a lifetime, your memories and knowledge are, for the most part, shut off from you, so you can live this life and learn on a very real level.

If you are about to commit an act, whether it is moral, honorable, unethical, or downright illegal, you may feel a strong emotion concerning this upcoming act. This is your higher mind guiding you, but it could also be that you are sub-consciously remembering a past life event, and drawing on the lessons learned from it. The ***Universal Law of Karma***—you will receive what you put in, and as you sow then so shall you reap. This law has had a major impact on your past lives, and will do the same in your future lives. The ***Universal Law of Incarnation Characteristics***— your past lifetimes have formed certain personality traits that you have now. A good example is to analyze why children have different attitudes and behavioral characteristics even when they are raised in the same environmental settings. Your past lives will also determine situational experiences that you may face in your next lifetime. Past lives will form bonds with other spirits who become your soulmates. Also, past lives sub-consciously form your viewpoint on issues.

Review these examples:

- In a prior lifetime, you killed and tortured a person. Now in this lifetime, you will assist that spirit that you mistreated or even experience the treatment you served upon that person. What goes around comes around! The ***Law of Karma*** is in play here.

- In a prior lifetime, you were in a terrible war and never had peace; now in this lifetime, you seek peace and fulfillment. When this idea is threatened, you over-react to the threat in comparison to what an average person would. This is an example of how past lifetimes form personality traits with the ***Universal Law of Incarnation Characteristics***.

- A previous lifetime of alcohol addiction may result in a spirit dependant on artificial stimulation. You now face another lifetime of potential substance abuse, which has to be overcome in order to grow. The addiction will be overcome, whether it is in this lifetime or the next, no matter how many lifetimes it takes. The life situational experience of addiction here.

- In this lifetime, you warm very quickly to a new friend, or become intimate with a partner and feel a connection. This is most likely you connecting with your soul mate.

- You may also find yourself drawn to episodes in history and even feeling a pull towards one side of a conflict: say the French army in World War II, or the Germanic tribes fighting against the Roman Empire. Your viewpoint on issues here is your higher mind recalling past life events that you experienced.

The spirit, in consultation with the heavenly guides, chooses the lifetime lessons. Your soulmates are spirits whom you have bonded with previously in heaven or in a living dimension, and your lifetime, in general, prior to birth. So, you choose all these previous lifetimes for a reason: to learn the lesson and to grow. Yes, that is right. We choose our life experiences. People may say: "What? I chose this mess?" You probably did to experience the sensation, or you created the mess by the decisions you have made so far in your lifetime. Just as there are no bad lifetimes, there are no bad decisions, only decisions that will result in learning for you in one way or another.

Remember, we can't turn past life memories on and off like tap water while we are in physical form, because it would nullify the learning effect of this lifetime, but when you are told an event from a past lifetime, you will know it in your soul. The memories are there in your higher mind and, occasionally, through mediation, you will sense feelings and images that pertain to a previous lifetime, and you can gain counsel from your higher mind from this.

You may be a little apprehensive about previous lifetimes; for example, finding out whom you were in previous lifetimes, or even worse, what you did! Do not be. It is the essence of your existence to learn the ways of the universe and grow. A practicing psychic counselor who offers past life readings, or your own mediation and opening of the higher mind should be able give you insights into your past life experiences.

- You may be shocked to find out that you were a soldier on the wrong side in WWII. Remember, in those days, either you obeyed the draft or you were shot.

- You may find out that you were a member of the opposite sex. All sprits in the universe are the same energy field: so there is no male and female in heaven, just spirits. This universal truth can take a while to really sink in and to understand.

- You are a farm worker content in your ways in this life. You were in another lifetime a CEO of steel company in the early 20th Century. You may feel that you are going backwards now. No, you are not. You had different choices then, and now you choose to work with the earth's natural environment in this lifetime for different reasons too.

- You may have had a lifetime and learned very little for yourself, but this was preordained, as your purpose was to help another spirit achieve a difficult goal. This is quite common when we have spirits incarnate purely to help others.

There are no bad lifetimes of learning, only just learning experiences. Now let's pause here and read—not all serious criminal activity is part of a spirit's learning journey. Theft, rape, cold-blooded murder, unnecessary wars, and conflicts, to name but a few are not permitted activities of learning.

Remember though that past lives are what they are: past. What is done is done, and cannot be undone. Open your mind, learn from the memories, and accept them for what they are.

As I grew up and started becoming more universally aware, I felt as if I had a few lifetimes before this one. I sought guidance on this and visited a very loving, gifted, and well-known psychic lady counselor in 1999 in Arlington, TX, by the name of Leona Mayers. I was interested in the spiritual universe from a young age and she confirmed that my thoughts and feelings were true on many matters, including past lives. From a young age, I was deeply interested in the Roman Empire, Judea, American Indians, the Titanic, and World War II. Leona conducted a past-life reading and confirmed my feelings and other amazing events in my spirit's journey. The second time I visited with Leona, I sensed that I had known her from a previous lifetime, and even she, later on in our friendship, commented on this in a casual conversation. I know now, through my own intuition, that I was meant to be guided by Leona and my cousin, Stephen Adair, in this lifetime.

Part 2

Chapter Summary Points

A Lifetime: You are here on Earth with the objective to learn and understand God's ways through universal learning. You will undertake this universal learning by experiencing emotional and life experiences for spiritual growth.

Emotional and Life Experiences: We have to learn the emotional and life experiences that Earth living can offer, such as love, fear, integrity, and hardship, to name a few. The lessons we undertake to experience must truly be learned.

The Life Path: You chose how your life would evolve in order for you to engage in the learning experiences. This will become the life path for you once you incarnate into the living dimension.

The Natural Ending: When our physical existence ceases on planet Earth, our eternal spirit leaves this living dimension and returns to the heavenly spiritual dimension where it belongs.

Past lifetimes: These are your previous lifetimes as a life form. The memories of these lifetimes are stored in your higher mind, and your soul has absorbed the emotional feeling associated with events of such lifetimes.

Part 3

How to Achieve Success and Fulfillment in your Lifetime of Universal Learning

Now you know who you are and why you are here on Earth. In your lifetime, you now desire to achieve success and fulfillment in whatever path you have chosen.

We say success in terms of trying and learning. We say fulfillment can be the state of contentment of the spirit when the lifetime is manifesting itself to the chosen path of learning, and the general state of being truly happy.

In part 3, we shall start with the known living universe, planet Earth, and the reality of living on it. Then discuss inner and outer guidance, followed by relationships. We will then progress on to setting goals and overcoming obstacles. Harnessing the power of life will be next, and we will conclude part 3 with a discussion about success and failure.

Chapter 10

The Living Universe, Earth, and the Reality of Living on the Planet

To achieve success and fulfillment in your life, you need to have a sense of awareness of where you physically are in this dimension. We are currently not in the spiritual dimension, which is our natural home. We are here in the Milky Way Galaxy and on planet Earth. Therefore, an understanding of the living universe, planet Earth, and the truthful reality of living on it, is necessary. We discussed, earlier in the book, that if we do not have the truth, coupled with some sense of reality, it will be difficult for us to achieve our goals because we will not know where we are to begin.

The Living Universe

The Earth is part of the Milky Way galaxy and the known living universe. This universe is a living dimension of divine creation. The living dimensions are endless, so their sizes are immeasurable. Let's put this knowledge into perspective somewhat.

Based on our current knowledge of astronomy, the Milky Way Galaxy contains approximately 400 billion stars: four hundred billion, hot, glowing, gas balls! Not forgetting the sun in our solar system, which we consider the be all and end all, as it warms us and sustains planetary life, is only one of these: only one! Astronomers estimate that there are approximately

125 billion galaxies in the known universe and they estimate the number of stars to be 1×10^{22}: this equates to one plus twenty-two zeros. Now that is a lot of stars! These figures are based on what we know at this time in human development. Makes you think, doesn't it?

Modern science has advanced greatly in the last 100 years and has accumulated more data to confirm their hypothesis of universal creation, with big bang theories and so on. These discoveries are amazing, and the scientific communities have my admiration and utmost respect. Because of scientific advancement, many people are now asking the question: "Did God really create this universe and our world?" Some claim the big bang theory happened over 13 billion years ago, and the perception of God and divine creation is irrelevant because it was too long ago for Him to be involved. Well, let me ask you two simple questions: "Who exactly created this Big Bang and why?" I will respectfully answer them for you: "God did." Remember, there is no time in the spiritual universe and formation of galaxies and dimensions can take as long as they need.

There are other planets in the living universe that contain life forms, millions of them—life forms of all shapes and sizes, from microbes to humanoid types, to bizarre-looking masses. Don't be afraid of other life forms, there is no need to be. In time, the knowledge of extraterrestrial life forms will be made public.

Our known living dimension, with its quadrillions of stars, is only one dimension! Only one out of how many living dimensional planes? Now, you are in awe, as you should be. Hopefully, you have a little more understanding and comprehension of the infinite universal living dimensions now.

The Planet Earth

The Earth is the fifth largest of nine planets in our solar system. The Sun is 92,897,000 miles from Earth and the planet is moving through space at 45,000 m.p.h. The diameter of our planet, when measured around the equator, is nearly 8,000 miles. The age of the Earth is estimated to be 4.65 billion years old, and currently contains over 2 million known species, ranging in size from microscopic organisms to whales. All these life forms contain an eternal energy that is their spirit, and all these life forms reside on this world with us.

To say that God created this planet is true, as all in the living dimensions were created by His doing, and all flows back to the source, Him. All things, from the first microbes of life on Earth to your physical body, were created by God. People may say, "What about Charles Darwin's theory on Natural Selection?" Yes, this theory is most true, and it all sources back to the first microbe of life on Earth 4 billion years ago, which was created by the Big Bang, which was created by God. There is much to discover and learn about the living universe from a human scientific perspective, but there is no avoiding the universal creator--God, the heavenly father.

Our world is a stunningly beautiful planet full of natural resources and brimming with life. However, the reality of life on Earth is a mixture of wonder and disappointment. There is a serious amount of damage being done to Earth's environment and exhaustion of resources by humankind. This must be balanced. It took billions of years to form the Earth's present day environment and resources, and we just can't squander them in two or three-hundred years. We must learn to respect nature. After all, it is what sustains us, and we need Mother Earth more than she needs us. The Earth is a living breathing planet and Mother Nature is be respected. I caution you, the Universal ***Law of Karma*** works for all; do not underestimate Mother Nature. Taking universal laws aside, there are natural disasters that can strike at any given moment, which can produce tragic results. This is a consequence of incarnating onto a living, breathing planet. The living dimensions are a training ground, not a perfect heavenly sanctuary.

The Earth is an amazing place for a spirit to incarnate onto to learn lessons, because of the natural environment and many diverse human cultures and societies. You and I chose to incarnate into this world and there is no denying this: you are reading this text are you not?

The Reality of Life on Earth

Mankind has made great advances on Earth, such as healthcare, technology, and space exploration. Peoples' lives are generally healthier, and living conditions are improving. In First World countries, people enjoy a high standard of living, provided they work for it. We have brought nations together in trade and world development and we are now considered a global community.

However, despite this good progress, mankind has still to eradicate very serious problems such as:

- Famine, disease, conflict, and diabolical human rights violations are problems that have been around since recorded time began.

- We have evil, tyrannical, and despotic regimes still in the world.

- We have totally unjustifiable, purely evil acts of terrorism, which are committed almost on a daily basis.

- We have major criminal activity in the world.

- Our moral and ethical standards are all over the place and people don't know what is right or wrong in this regard anymore. For example: frivolous lawsuits, get-rich quick scams, financial deception, and inappropriate viewing of media content available to young children.

Those who kill innocent people in the name of religion are no different that any other who commits a cold-blooded murder, and they will pay for every ounce of suffering they have caused by experiencing it themselves through the **Universal law of Karma**. I can assure you this will happen to all those who commit cold-blooded murder.

The world is going through a tremendous change in awareness and knowledge, and the fear of change can be traumatic for governments and people. Nations are currently no more than a bunch of squabbling children who are always trying to dominate each other economically and culturally, and who could not agree on the color of the ocean on a sunny day.

Many people say that money is the root of all evil. They say that most criminal acts and unethical conduct in business, is attributed to greed. Well, the reality of life on Earth is that money does not commit crimes. It does not rob banks, nor does it cook the books at a Fortune 500 company—human beings do these things—not money. Money and wealth may corrupt you if you let them, but the choice is yours. They can also be of great benefit.

All of the above is the reality of modern day life on Earth. Many people fall into the negative side of the **Universal Law of Emotional Control** and give in to fear, anger, and hate, and commit many of the above listed, and that is why it is important to correlate the reality of life with the universal laws to make people aware of the error of their ways.

Despite these problems, there are more good people than bad ones, better honest nations than despotic regimes, and more desire to bring the world together. In times to come, our world will learn to live as one free people, living peacefully with one another and the planet. In the not so distant future, mankind may realize the awesome potential of exploring the living universe: meaning space exploration and colonization. We can and will achieve this much quicker than you may think, providing we do not annihilate ourselves with the deadly weapons we now possess. Now the pessimists amongst us will say, "This will never happen, it's too far to travel, and we can't do it." I say, "really?" Please review the following:

You cannot sail around the world

Ferdinand Magellan was a Portuguese-born, Spanish explorer and navigator. He was credited as the leader of an expedition in 1519, which sailed completely around the world.

Man cannot fly

On December 17, 1903, in North Carolina, the now-famous brothers, Wilbur and Orville Wright, made the world's first successful flight in a heavier-than-air craft under power and control.

The sound barrier will never be broken

On October 14, 1947, in California, Chuck Yeager flew the X-1 experimental aircraft to a speed of 1065 km/h (662 mph), faster than the speed of sound.

You will never land a man on the moon

On July 16, 1969, Neil Armstrong and Edwin Aldrin, who were part of the Apollo 11 mission, stepped off the lunar module onto the moon's surface.

The above four examples are related to exploration. Human beings will always strive to overcome difficulties and achieve new objectives. The essence of our spirits is to seek out and learn. There is no stopping us. We thrive on achievement. The spirit will always advance in learning, no matter how many attempts, or how long it takes.

Chapter 11

Inner Guidance

Why do we need to have inner guidance you may ask? By seeking out inner spiritual guidance you will be helping yourself achieve success and fulfillment in your life. Guidance from the spiritual universe and your own higher mind can only help you. In seeking inner guidance, you will open your mind and your life to new possibilities. Remember the Universal *Law of Action & Effect:* seek and you shall find.

Inner guidance is a process of consultation between your normal consciousness and your higher mind. Your higher mind is your conduit to the spiritual universe. Your spirit consists of a soul and a higher mind, which are inseparable, as they are the same thing. The soul absorbs all the emotional experiences and your higher mind is the brain of the spirit containing all memories and knowledge of all that is, and all that has been learned by you so far in your universal existence.

By seeking inner guidance, you are asking for counsel and assistance in your lifetime. You may ask the question: "Who am I seeking guidance from?" You are seeking guidance from God, the spiritual universe, your guides, and your higher mind (Quite an impressive line up, wouldn't you say?). Inner guidance is practiced mostly with meditation and prayer in order to access and consult with your higher mind and the aforementioned. You may ask, "Why can't I consult right now and get all the answers I need?" If you did that and accessed all the answers of the universe, then what would be the point of this life of real-time learning?

To access your higher mind normally requires practicing regular meditation. To the beginner this may seem a little weird and a load of hocus pocus rubbish. However, I can assure you that meditation is very simple to do and enjoyable. Some readers may be regular users of meditation and other relaxation techniques. If you're a beginner and would like to start opening your mind by practicing regular meditation and have no clear idea of how to start practicing basic meditation, then try the following simple exercise to start opening your awareness. Prior to each meditation always say a prayer asking God for guidance and for his love and protection during meditation: you can ask for this in any manner you deem appropriate to your beliefs:

Step 1 Find a quite spot in your place of dwelling where you will be undisturbed for a while. Sit down in a chair or other item of furniture that allows you to be comfortable, and make sure your spine is fairly straight.

Step 2 Once you are positioned and comfortable, loosely focus your vision on a spot in front of you, relax, and allow your mind to quiet down. Breathe slowly and fully without forcing anything. Just relax and enjoy the peace and quiet. Remember to keep your thoughts as still as you can.

Step 3 Now, while you are enjoying the quietness, breathing at a regular pace, and feeling more relaxed, you can close your eyes. Remember to keep breathing at the same pace and keep your mind quiet. Thoughts may come and go, but be loosely focused on just breathing and achieving a quiet state of mind. Try to keep this peaceful state of mind for at least 15-30 minutes and when you are ready to finish, take two or three deep breaths and slowly open your eyes. When you feel alert and focused, you may return to your normal daily activities.

The above exercise is a simple meditation technique that enables you to feel relaxed, calm, and refreshed. Regular meditation starts to open the spiritual energy within and around you. Achieving the flow of energy through you is most beneficial, as energy is the endless life force of this entire universe. There are many more meditation and relaxation techniques that we can do, but that is not the intention of this particular book. Meditation and psychic counsel will be written in more depth in later books in the series.

Once you start meditating on a regular basis, let's say three or four times a week, you can start doing some simple affirmations near the end of each meditation. Affirmations are positive declarations you are making to your higher mind, which, in turn, will affect your conscious life. You will be amazed at how much stating positive affirmations can improve the quality off your life. Here are some simple affirmations to get you started. Say each of the affirmations three times aloud to yourself just before you end your meditation:

- I am now at peace with myself, and I open my higher mind to the energy and guidance of the universe.

- I am now more energetic, healthier, and positive in my life.

- I am now tuning into my higher purpose in my lifetime, and my goals of universal learning.

- I am now manifesting those things that will benefit me in my lifetime, as it was meant to be.

These simple affirmations will start to increase your awareness of the power of visualization and positive thinking and will embark you on a journey of enlightenment. You may not notice the results the next day, but look back a month from now and ask yourself: "Do I feel better about life?"

By meditating and stating positive affirmations, you'll be developing your higher mind and increasing your awareness and intuition: this all works with the ***Universal Law of Guidance***. Let go of the negative emotions, slow your mind down, and let the energy of the universe that flows around you, bring you all the information you need at this point in your lifetime.

Remember, everything in the living and spiritual universe consists of energy—ALL OF IT! When I used to hear the term "energy," when I was younger, I shrugged it off and thought, "Whatever," but now it is so clear to me. We are spirits who are composed of pure energy and we connect with other forms of energy, whether it is a leather football or feeling the emotion of love. We as spirits of energy which were created by the superior spirit-God are all capable of so much if we only open our minds and listen. Some people may think that money (which is still pretty cool to have) is the life force of the world, it is not. The feeling of fulfillment and happiness in life is from emotional energy and not green faced bills. When you pass from this current lifetime, you cannot take your money and possessions with you. So, what you take with you is what you have learned, which is stored in your higher mind and in the form of; what? Energy.

By meditating and saying positive affirmations, you will be accessing the flow of energy, which is the vehicle of all in existence in the spiritual and living universe. Do not be apprehensive at all about meditating, as it can only help you. Achieving a calm, clear, focused state of mind will enable you to achieve a lot more in life than you realize; and your guides will find it easier to assist you as you open up sub-consciously to them. You may find that you understand matters more and that things in life start falling into place a little easier for you once you start accessing the universal energy that is flowing around the planet Earth and yourself. Although I would respectfully caution you, don't spend your entire life meditating and flower powering your way around.

Get up and get into the action of modern-day life, but take time out to reconnect with your inner-self through meditation, and keep on saying positive affirmations.

Every night when we sleep, we dream. One of the benefits of dreams is that your higher mind receives guidance from the universe through the dream state. Dreams can be interpreted in many different ways: there are many specialized books on the subject. We dream about:

- Past lives
- Our spiritual home
- Past love ones
- Current events in our life
- Our fears
- Possible future outcomes
- General guidance from the universe

Many people in the world use prayer as a form of inner guidance. As we have said, everything in the universe is energy. People pray in many different forms, to many different religions and beliefs. It is their right as human beings and spirits of God's universe to worship and pray in any fashion they desire.

In my lifetime, I have ascertained that meditating and stating positive affirmations is extremely beneficial. My only regret is that I wish I had started doing it 20 years ago.

Chapter 12

Outer Guidance

Outer guidance is the process of consultation between yourself and the people or organizations of our world. We seek outer guidance on a daily basis, whether we realize this or not. Religion, family and friends, and even psychic counsel can serve as good forms of guidance for us.

Religion plays a major part in people's lives as a form of outer guidance. We classify religion as outer guidance because it focuses primarily on interconnection with the outside world: in terms of people and organizations. However, we all appreciate that people take religion inwardly, therefore it can also be grouped as a form of inner guidance. Religion is belief in a supreme being or beings: belief in God or Gods.

Many follow a religion because it's part of their family or tribal heritage and culture. For others, religion provides a feeling of security, because the divine power is believed to be watching over them and religion promises salvation and life after death. For other people, religion yields a sense of individual fulfillment and provides meaning to life.

Major recognizable and popular religions and beliefs are:

Buddhism--founded in northeastern India and based on the teachings of Siddhartha Gautama, who is known as the Buddha, or Enlightened One.

Christianity--based on the teachings of Jesus Christ of Nazareth. Christianity is the most widely distributed of the world religions.

Hinduism--originated in India and is still practiced by most of its inhabitants. Hinduism is basically defined by what people do rather than what they think.

Islam--central teaching is that there is only one all-powerful, all-knowing God, and this God created the universe.

Judaism--religious culture of the Jews (people of Israel) is one of the world's oldest continuing religions.

Shinto--Japanese cult and religion, originating in prehistoric times, and occupying an important national position for long periods in the history of Japan, particularly in recent times.

New Age--broad-based amalgam of diverse spiritual, social, and political elements with the common aim of transforming individuals and society through spiritual awareness.

Sikhism-- centered in Punjab State, in northwestern India. Sikhism is an ethical monotheism fusing elements of Hinduism and Islam.

For many people, religion and beliefs are ceremonies, practices, and worship involving a supreme God(s) or Deity.

Almost all people who follow some form of religion or belief, believe that a supreme being(s) created the world and influences their current lives.

I wish to state clearly for you once again that you are free to worship or believe any religion or faith you choose. You should never be discriminated against or discriminate against anyone else for their belief system—period. Those who harm and claim their deed in the name of God or any religion are false—for every ounce of harm they cause they shall receive in turn as per the **Universal Law of Karma**. Do not blame God, religions, or beliefs for the acts of violence and evil doings of an individual or a few as per the **Universal Law of Free Will** and the **Universal Law of Action & Effect**. Religions, beliefs, and faith are very comforting for the people of this world and are a great source of outer guidance. There are many paths to God and all must be respected and honored—no one earthly religion or belief is better than another. The people of the world need to be more tolerant of each other and religious beliefs. We have shed too much blood over religious ideology; which is supposed to preach love, peace, and compassion in the first place!

A different form of outer guidance in a lifetime on Earth is consulting with family and friends; they can give general sound and solid advice on matters that trouble us from time to time. Consult with the elders of your family, people with experience as the old saying: "Age breeds wisdom," is most true.

Another good source of outer guidance is to consult with a professional psychic counselor who practices in life purpose readings and possible future outcomes. Some people doubt the power of psychic readings and other metaphysical forms of counseling. I can assure you they will not doubt after their first reading. The people that practice in this field are no different than any other human being, except they have mastered, to some degree, accessing the energy flow of this living universe These gifted people are able to do much good work for the planet and all its inhabitants. They basically receive and interpret information given from God and the guides for you for your lifetime—it is as simple as that. They only tell you what you need to know at a specific point in time, in order for you to learn and make the most of your lifetime on Earth.

I consulted with a few psychic practitioners as my fascination with the studies of the metaphysical universe grew. I found the information from psychic counselors valuable and totally fascinating.

Chapter 13

Relationships

Our relationships with family, friends, and people in general, can bring us an enormous amount happiness and fulfillment. Relationships are critical in our spiritual development during our lifetime on Earth as we experience and learn so much because of them. Whether our relationships turn out good or bad it matters only that you truly appreciate and learn from them.

Some may ask the question, "Why do we need relationships? I dislike my family and hate my ex-husband, so I don't need anyone." True, you may not physically need anyone in your post childhood life, but are you happy, fulfilled, and content? If you interact with no one or do not have the desire too, then you probably will become a lonely, bitter, depressed person. "Why is that then?" you may ask. Because in life there really is only one thing that makes a person happy and that is another person. Sure, we all say a million dollars will make us happy and fulfilled—is that so? Well, look at the example in the following paragraph:

- You pick up your net check from the Power-Ball Lottery and it is for $740,337.67 Yehaa! So you go immediately to the BMW car dealership and you trade in your existing vehicle and pay cash for that 3-Series convertible you deeply desired. You are driving down the street in your brand spanking new wheels and you are so excited that you bought this car for which you have yearned. The feeling is great and you want to share your joy. You want to tell people of your joy, but you have no one to call as you do not have any meaningful relationships with any other human beings. The novelty of the new car wears off in time and the feeling of emptiness returns to your life. Now it sinks in that you do really need relationships as your new money and car does not replace the value of having a good relationship with another human being.

We do need fulfilling relationships in our lifetimes; these can be with our family, friends, and the general public. Remember, we are free to choose whom we have our special and fulfilling relationships with. You do not have to tolerate any type of destructive, hurtful, or unfulfilling relationship with any person or thing—suffer on the account of no one.

Let me tell you the most important relationship you will ever have during your lifetime on Earth: **the one with yourself!** If you cannot achieve a sense of enjoyment and fulfillment from your own life, how are you going to have successful relationships with others? If you are unhappy and you choose to remain unhappy, negative, and bitter about past events in your life—the *Universal Law of Free Will*— then you may find that this unhappiness you have within your own life will spread into other relationships and your life in general. People will slowly, but surely, not want to deal with you, as you are perceived to be negative and unattractive to be around. I bring this to your attention because so many people don't realize that what you think about, whether it is positive or negative, other people pick up on, regardless of their spiritual or psychic stage of development. Ever hear someone say, "I don't get good vibes from that person?" That is their higher mind informing them that this person or thing may not be such a good idea right now—the *Universal of Guidance.* You normally get these feelings on bad first dates—I speak from experience.

The plain fact is that your life is for you to learn. However, there are a few spirits who live purely for the benefit of others: albeit a tiny fraction of the Earth's population. You are here to learn for you, and in order to do that you need to have a good relationship with your lifetime on Earth: **you need to have a good relationship with yourself first and foremost**. If you are struggling a little, don't worry, we will discuss overcoming obstacles in life later on. Remember, if you knew it all about learning and lifetimes, then you would not be here, nor would I.

Your family, friends, and your general relationships with the outside world can give you much satisfaction, fulfillment, and joy—the **Universal law of Love.** Memories from your relationships can last a lifetime and be a source of great comfort. However, relationships can also bring you much heartbreak and sadness. Let me give you a solid piece of advice; don't bother to have relationships with people who hurt you or abuse you in any way, shape, or form, no matter who they are; your mother, father, or any of your family members, including grown-up children, and so on.

Relationships teach us so much in life, because most, if not all types of relationships draw on emotions. Many of the lessons we chose to experience in life relate to emotions, as we listed in chapter 6, such as love, compassion, contentment— also jealousy, anger, and hate. Relationships really test our observance of the universal laws as emotions can and do push us to the limits, as our experiences in life draw on our emotional power. The universal laws are applicable to everyone and everything in existence and are there to be observed. As you know, we humans have a hard time controlling our emotions. Controlling one's emotions is critical in life, as we cannot turn back the clock after an unnecessary emotional loss of control—the **Universal Law of Emotional Control**.

You literally have thousands of relationships in your life. How you treat each relationship will determine how your life will develop and how much you learn in your lifetime. You now may be asking the question, "So, how do I get the best out of my relationships?"

When reviewing our relationships in life, we need to analyze and evaluate the following points:

1. Who are we having relationships with?

2. Are they positive or negative relationships?

3. What emotional experiences are usually associated   with each relationship?

4. Are we observing the universal laws during such relationships?

You may find the answers quite revealing in a good or not so good way. However, identification with reality with relationships, or anything in life, is critical to pursuing success and fulfillment. In the following paragraph there are some general pointers for having satisfying and fulfilling relationships.

Be **respectful, courteous, and ethical** in your conduct towards people. Manners cost nothing. Treat people how you want to be treated. **Never be quick to judge** people, regardless of what they believe, or what they do for a living. Remember the 2000 year-old story about the man who was a carpenter? **Open your mind** to other people's opinions, as you may learn something new and they, like us, have a right to be heard. Give people the **benefit of the doubt** and let them live and learn: no one gets it right the first time all the time. Be **totally honest** with yourself and others, so you will know where you are in a relationship.

To get anywhere with anything, you need to know where you are in order to begin. Learn to **communicate** and **control your emotions**, especially any rash temper tantrums, saying "I'm sorry" sometimes cannot repair damage to one's credibility. **Set goals** for your relationships, as you need something for which to aim. **Learn to give and take** in relationships, be there for each other. **Retain your original identity** and your own personal goals and desires, and don't let others impose their selfish ways on you. They were attracted to you because of who and what you are and not what you can become. Do not give into **fear, jealousy, anger,** etc. as they will dominate your relationships and eventually destroy them. Remember, you are allowed to experience these emotions, but learn to control them. Do not **involve yourself in destructful relationships**; take abuse from no one. Learn to **forgive and forget**, especially the forgetting part. Seek out fulfilling relationships and not shallow ones. Most importantly, **learn from your relationships**.

You must interact with those who will bring you happiness, success, and fulfillment. There is a saying that you become like those who you associate with, this is quite true. You can help, guide, and comfort those who seek the same happiness as you. Relationships are not a bed of roses and you cannot hire and fire folks that you have relationships with on an hourly basis, but as I have said, do not suffer disrespectful treatment from anyone.

You will find as you grow in your lifetime that friends, lovers, and hopefully, not too many marriages, will come and go. This is because the relationships we have with each other serve a higher purpose at all levels. Many of the relationships we have in our lifetimes are preordained. These relationships were orchestrated by all the relevant spirits and guides prior to the lifetime for the benefit of each spirit's goals of universal learning. For example:

- You may have chosen to help a spirit experience a tough childhood and be a close friend during this, but when the relevant time came and the lesson was completed, you moved on to a separate life path. All things, including relationships, end, and there is a purpose for it all.

I could write a 750-page book about the relationships I have had in my life journey so far. These relationships were good and bad experiences, but the main thing is that I learned from them.

Chapter 14

Set Goals & Work to Achieve Them

By setting goals for yourself and working towards them, you achieve success and fulfillment in life. Furthermore, you will manifest your lifetime towards your chosen path of learning. You will learn lessons in life no matter what, but by setting goals and objectives you will be more likely to fulfill your destiny, and your preordained learning experiences will be more forthcoming. The **Universal Law of Action and Effect** states that no action (goal setting) will result in no effect (learning). You will be following your chosen life path more as a result of setting goals and working towards them.

You may ask the question, "How I am supposed to know what to choose: what goals, when, and how do I achieve them?" What do you desire and what do you want to be in your life? What are your dreams? Let these thoughts flow around in your mind for a few minutes.

You may feel that you do not need to set goals in your life and everything is great—wrong! Every moment of your existence is spent creating and achieving goals, such as getting up in the morning and setting a goal to arrive at work or school on time, which can be difficult at times; however these are everyday normal goals. When we refer to goals, it is in the context of love, family, career, and destiny, for example. As the spirit thrives on learning, you will feel uneasy and unsettled if you don't have goals and objectives in your life. You know what happens when you don't have anything to work towards? Nothing.

A life of a human being without goals and objectives is like a lost ship at sea. As you are now living your life, you are at sea, and sailing along in the journey of life. You left port the day you were born, with the destination of experiencing preordained events and learning lessons. Your lessons and experiences will come as you live your life, but if you have no will—the ***Universal law of Free Will***— to work at developing and learning, you will become lost. The reason you will become lost is because you have no destination (goals). Without a clear goal, you will probably not experience your preordained events and learn from them—the ***Universal Law of Preordination.*** It is like all the equipment working on the vessel (your life), but the captain (you) has not given the final order for the destination coordinates. The ship is sailing without direction, but hopefully, the captain (you) may realize this and set course for land (by working towards goals), and find such land (experience lessons) someday. Alternatively, the ship may never reach land and will sail aimlessly at sea, due to the decisions of the captain (you).

You may think, "Alright, but I will choose any goals I want, regardless of my preordained life path I chose prior to incarnation. Yes, it is true that in life you can achieve almost anything you want if you are willing to work and sacrifice for it. However, you will feel uneasy and unfulfilled if you spend your life working towards a goal that you do not truly and deeply believe in, or that is not part of your life plan prior to birth. So far, you have read in this book that by avoiding your true life path and its relevant lessons you will have to face the same lessons in a future lifetime. Remember, we have an eternity's worth of time to learn—the ***Universal Law of Time.***

In any lifetime, anywhere in the universe, you will get absolutely nowhere if you don't work for it—the ***Universal Law of Action & Effect***—life owes you nothing, no matter who you are or where you came from—you owe God for this life, so start working for it. We say "work for it" as the general application of effort to achieve something: getting up in the morning and trying! Whining, complaining, and being lazy are not applying effort to reach a goal. No action will equate to no effect.

This brings us back to the question asked in the second paragraph about what goals you should choose and how you can achieve them. Let's do the following very simple example exercise:

Step 1—Identify your Goals

Ask yourself the following questions in order to identify your goals.

- Where do you want to live?
- What do want to do in your life?
- What do you want to be?

These three questions can bring up a lot of answers, but that is fine. Just make a mental note of your thoughts and allow the information to flow around in your mind. You may not be aware of it, but you are probably being coached by your guides in making decisions here to help you achieve the lessons you are meant to learn.

Step 2 – Write your goals on paper

When you have decided what goals you want to achieve, write them down on paper or type them on your PC. Now you have started to really commit to them by making the effort to write about them. The desire to achieve these goals will start to manifest itself in your mind. Let's create three hypothetical goals:

1. Move to San Francisco
2. Get the promotion to Vice President
3. Become a better tennis payer

Step 3 – How are you going to achieve your goals?

Now, you are looking at your list of goals and wondering how you will achieve this. Make a few notes beside each goal about steps or actions you can take to achieve that goal, for example:

1. Move to San Francisco – request a branch transfer
2. Get the promotion to Vice President – successfully complete a master's degree with the University of Phoenix
3. Become a better tennis payer – take lessons at the club

Step 4 – Set target dates

You have to set target dates for completion of your goal, because if you do not, they probably will not get done. If you cannot commit to a completion date, then you are not seriously committed to achieving the goal.

1. Move to San Francisco – request a branch transfer: submit on 06/01/2005
2. Get the promotion to Vice President – successfully complete a master's degree with University of Phoenix: enroll by the end of July 2005
3. Become a better tennis payer – get lessons at the club: call Pat Waddell by 05/01/2005

Step 5 – Work towards your goal and review your progress

Now that you have set target dates to start or complete your goals, you need to work at them. You will have hiccups and distractions along the way, but remain committed and keep working at it. Never forget the reason why you desired to achieve this goal.

Review your progress, commend yourself for achieving your goals, and most importantly, for giving yourself the opportunity to learn along the way. Your existence is to learn. You see how we keep referring back to the same phrases; learning, lessons, and universal laws.

To achieving success and fulfillment in your life, it is imperative to set goals and achieve them. To be successful at anything is good, and the fulfillment of achieving a goal is a wonderful and satisfying feeling.

In my lifetime, I set a goal for myself to live in the United States of America. Since I was a young boy, I have always had a deep desire to live here in the USA and become a citizen. Now I look back on my life and I realize it was part of my destiny to achieve this. However, make no mistake; I had to work for it!

The childhood idea of this goal was finally set in motion while I was a resident of South Africa in 1995. I knew I needed business-related educational qualifications to compliment my trade and technical qualifications. I embarked on a diploma in business studies, which I successfully completed in 1997. That same year, I left South Africa and returned to the United Kingdom to prepare and fulfill my burning desire to live and work in the USA. From projects I worked on in South Africa, I knew a gentleman who owned a specialty contracting company in Texas and he was kind enough to apply to the INS for an H-1B visa in the early part of 1998. On January 4, 1999, I stepped off a Continental Airlines flight in Houston, Texas, to become a legal, working resident of the United States of America—it was a feeling of total fulfillment.

Chapter 15

Overcoming Obstacles

During your lifetime, you are going to have to overcome many obstacles to achieve success and fulfillment. We will discuss some common obstacles that we face in our lifetimes that can hold us back:

Broken Family

Many people, including myself, come from a broken family, meaning our parents divorced or separated when we were children. Some of us were even more unfortunate in that we had a parent pass from this Earth during our childhood.

Many children grow up angry and bitter towards their parents for the trauma and sadness they were put through. It is most true to say that the children of any broken marriage tend to suffer the most, so you it is of no surprise that many children from broken marriages tend to feel a little sad and bitter about their past. For those of you who feel this way, learn to show empathy towards your parents and imagine yourself in their shoes and relate this to the ***Universal Law of Love.*** Sometimes, there are circumstances that warrant parents to separate. I do not think there are many parents in the world that separated and divorced and were happy that they caused their children such suffering.

Many children grow up living in the past and desire their parents to be reunited. What you need to understand is that it was your parents' choice to commit the acts they did and that was, and still is, their life and not yours. By constantly thinking about the events of the past, you are reliving and bringing to the forefront of your higher mind all of the negative emotions associated with the event, and you are putting yourself through the same pain again and again. Just remember, it wasn't you who caused the suffering; it was another, so don't feel guilty or ashamed. You must focus on your life now and let go of all the associated sadness related to being from a broken family—what is done is done and cannot be undone. Review what transpired, choose to learn from it, accept the lesson from the sadness, and move on.

Living in the Past

So many people live in the past, meaning they relate their current life right now to the events of the past and make all their decisions based on events that are done and cannot be undone. They strongly desire things to be the way they were. Change is inevitable and it is the only way to grow as per the ***Universal Law of Learning.*** How can you learn and grow if there is no change? It is imperative in life to realize that the past is quite literally the past.

Your lifetime is here and now, right now, as you're reading this book; it is not one, 10, or 20 years ago. However, if you are struggling in life and it is because of a past event that is holding you back, tell yourself: "My life begins here and now." Take whatever discomforting memories you hold and mentally put them in a box in a cupboard, and close the door. Don't forget about them; learn from them and move on.

Financial Hardship

Many people have a hard time overcoming financial hardships, as they believe it is their universal right to have money, quite simply, given to them and their lifestyles provided for them by the government. The government did not bring you into this world.

You volunteered for this lifetime! So, get up, take action, and provide for yourself. Much financial hardship is caused by not working at a job or other income-producing endeavor. Providing that you are mentally and physically able, you have no excuse for not having a job, especially in a country such as United States of America. There are millions of people in the world who would give anything to the legal right live and work here in the USA.

If you are too proud, or your pride prevents you from taking a low-paying job, even for a short time, then this is a problem and it needs to be overcome. Look at a person who works in a cornfield, for example. You may think he earns a pittance of a salary and you may view his or her existence in this world as trivial. I remind you that you cannot take your money and your possessions with you when you leave this world and return to your heavenly dimension. The worker in the cornfield may be more spiritually advanced than 95% of the earth's human population, so think twice before you judge anybody from a financial viewpoint. Life is not about money, it's about spiritual learning, and the man or woman who comes to the time of their passing with the most money does not win the game: that's not what this lifetime is about.

A life of hardship is normally caused by a person's own actions. The ***Universal Law of Action and Effect*** is applicable to all; there is no escape from it. If you choose a life of crime, drug addiction, or general laziness, then your results will be negative and you will only have yourself to blame. Do not blame society, your parents, or any other factor for any financial hardships you're experiencing now in your adult life. We all have the ability to be anything in life, if we are prepared to work for it. You need to be able to stand on your own two feet. You may say, "What about those people who inherit fortunes from their parents or other sources?" Their inheritance or their financial situation is none of your business. You should be concerned with **your** life and **your** financial situation.

Some of the world's most brilliant business people were born penniless. A plain fact of life is that in this world, you can have most anything if you are willing to work hard and sacrifice for it. Those who work hard and sacrifice for financial gain have the correct attitude, and attitude in modern-day life is everything.

Lack of Education

Many people have a lack of education, or they feel that they have a lack of education and are unable to succeed in the working world. If you did not complete high school, for example, or you did but had very poor grades and were unable or unwilling to attend places of further education, and you desire to improve yourself, then you must rectify the situation.

It is never, ever, too late in life to learn. Remember, life is about learning, from the moment you were born until the day you pass on, you learn all the way. It is the purpose of your spiritual existence to learn—so, get used to it.

You will achieve nothing by sitting at home in a chair, or sitting outside on the street looking cool and tough, whining and complaining about your lack of education and how hard a hand life has dealt you. You could be studying at home on a low-cost education program, which is extremely beneficial and fully transferable to all places of further education.

You may say, "I cannot afford education." You can obtain a recognizable 2-year degree in business management for $30 a month interest-free credit—$30 a month! If you cannot afford that small amount of money, then something is wrong. You must invest in yourself and your lifetime to bring success and fulfillment—the *Universal Law of Action & Effect.* Not only must you educate yourself academically, you must also learn the ways of life. No one is going to teach you a thing unless you try for yourself—you must make the effort.

I would also remind you that some of the most famous and distinguish CEOs and other prominent figures in the world were college dropouts. Therefore, a lack of education is not necessarily on obstacle. You may ask, "Why were these uneducated people successful?" They had the right attitude and they worked hard.

Physical and Other Disabilities

Some of you may have some physical and medical disabilities that prevent you from achieving what you desire in your lifetime.

You may be mentally and physically handicapped in your lifetime on Earth because you chose this experience for the growth and development of your spirit. On the other hand, you may just have had bad luck. Take heart that some of the most courageous people that this world has ever seen have been physically and mentally impaired, and they set a shining example for all those who have physical challenges to deal with during their lifetimes. They also set a disappointing contrast against those who do not have any disabilities but are just pure lazy and have a stinking attitude about life. Despite your disabilities and disadvantages in life, you can still give it your best shot, and when you leave this world you will know in your heart and soul that you truly lived.

Alcohol, Smoking, and Drug Addiction

You may have physical and mental addiction problems in your lifetime that are preventing you from achieving success and fulfillment. These are not inherent problems; you created them yourself, as we all do in our lifetime- the *Universal Law of Free Will*. These may be such things as alcohol and drug addiction, to name but a few. The harsh reality is that you created these problems by your actions and choices—The *Universal Law of Action & Effect*, but you can overcome these problems.

- In regards to alcohol addiction, **stop drinking**. "Just stop drinking?" You may say, "Oh, I can't do that." Why? Are you going to die if you do not drink alcohol? Consult with your doctor and just quit drinking. It is as simple as that. The reason you are drinking is that you probably have a serious problem in your life and you are deluding yourself: you are using alcohol as a source of comfort. This serious issue in your life needs to be overcome and worked through. Do not live in denial, we all have issues we have to work through and simply ignoring them or running away will not achieve a single thing—unfortunately this is the coldhearted truth.

- In regards to **drug addiction**, much of the above applies: get yourself checked into rehab and stick with it. "Easier said than done," some may say. Why is that so, do you want to be drug-free, yes or no? This may seem a little harsh, but folks, it's the only way. Yes or no, what's it going to be?

- People tell me that they desire to quit **smoking**. This is the same as alcohol and drug addiction. Don't talk about it, just do it. People say, "I will quit in a couple of weeks," or "I'm thinking about it," but they don't have the slightest intention to stop smoking; they are deluding themselves.

You will not find inner peace and fulfillment as long as you are seriously addicted to alcohol and or drugs. Your body, mentally and physically, cannot withstand daily abuse and you will not be in the physical condition to achieve much practical physical success in any application you choose to participate in. Will you?

Obesity

Many people in the world are overweight. They don't want to be in this state, but they are, and this can be personally embarrassing and traumatic for some of these people. Some people by their hereditary genes are built large and don't tend to mind having a few pounds and are quite happy, content, and fulfilled in life, and that's great. However, the vast majority of overweight people are not happy with their current situation. If you do not have a medical condition that's causing your weight problem, it all comes down to two simple factors. Just two--that's it:

- Eating habits—you are what you eat; it's as simple as that. There are many satisfying and enjoyable meals that are available in our stores that are very low-fat. For example; I eat many "Lean Cuisine" and "Healthy Choice" meals, much to the annoyance of my lovely wife who loves to cook for me. There are also many diets you can put yourself on, but if you are to go on a diet you need to stick to it! There is no point in participating in a top-quality diet program for six months and the going on the binge for six months. That is a total waste of time and energy. Just watch what you eat. It's as simple as that.

- Lack of physical exercise—in case you haven't noticed, the human body is mostly designed to run and hunt to survive. Believe it or not. Only in the last three to four hundred years, has civilization all but ended this way of life. So your body needs to walk or run. It needs to exercise to remain in peak condition. What happens when you're not in peak condition? You start to put on a little weight and generally feel unfit and lousy. Don't you? There are many top-quality fitness programs available at local health clubs and fitness centers, embark on one, as it will do you the world of good. Don't be afraid of how you look at the gym, no matter how overweight you are, don't succumb to fear— the *Universal Law of Emotional Control.*

It may seem hard to you, but you are overweight as a result of your actions—the *Universal Law of Action &Effect.* You know you can better your situation, so go ahead and do it.

Negative Emotions

Probably the biggest obstacle that human beings face is their own negative emotions. Fear, anger, hatred, and bitterness (to name but a few) are all common emotions to us. We have all experienced these emotions at least once in our lives. These negative emotions interact with the habits and challenges that we have discussed so far in this chapter.

You are allowed to experience these emotions. And you will experience them, but you must be able to control both your emotions and temperament—the *Universal Law of Emotional Control.*

- Fear is mankind's greatest enemy. We attack and destroy all things we do not understand. Fear holds many people back in life from doing the work that they came here to do. Fear of trying, fear of failure, and fear of ridicule are but a few examples of the fears that can hamper us in life. It is okay to be cautious and realistic; however, you must take risks in life in order to succeed. Do not let fear manipulate and control you.

- Anger must be controlled. A certain amount of anger can be good if it is funneled in a constructive and positive way. However, generally speaking, being angry is destructive to yourself and to those around you. Be honest with yourself and get to the root of the problem and solve your anger. Anger is often caused by the thoughts and emotions that we are holding within ourselves and not expressing. General frustrations build anxiety and anger within us. In all actuality, we are the problem and source of our anger and we need to find out how to solve it. Every problem in life can be resolved. For instance; you dislike your job. Well then, quit your job. You may say, "I need my job for the money." Get another one that pays, at least, the same.

- Hatred and Bitterness are the most destructive negative emotions you can possess, as hate will lead to total suffering—I can assure you.

- 1. Your high school sweetheart dumps you and runs off with your best friend. You hate them both for it and you become very bitter towards your high school memories because of them.

- 2. As a young child you were deprived of many things, as your father was an alcoholic. You become bitter towards your childhood memories and hateful towards your father for his drinking problems.

- 3. You may be so bitter that you criticize and ridicule everyone else about everything in order to make yourself feel better. All you are doing is driving people away. You will end up a lonely, truly bitter person.

Remember the past is the past and your life is here and now. Remembering, re-living, and torturing yourself with bad memories will not achieve a single constructive thing in your life. Let them go, learn from the experience, and move on.

Debris

Too often, people hold on to other people, things, and situations that no longer serve their highest good. This can apply to friends, family members, habits, personal belongings, ideas, beliefs, and careers.

There is no point in continuing relationships with people who exploit you, harm you, bring you unhappiness, or cast a negative shadow over your life. Just because they are family members or dear friends does not give them the right to conduct themselves in a manner that brings misery and unhappiness to your life. It requires great courage to confront, correct, or disassociate yourself with people whom you are close to in your life, but you must be willing to give yourself permission to let go of all that does not serve you. You cannot have a relationship with anyone who is causing your life to be miserable—why should you suffer on the account of another person's immoral, unethical, or abusive conduct?

If you have a habit, such as excessive smoking or drinking alcohol, that is hampering your happiness in life and you cannot seem to muster the courage to try and break such a habit, you must make the effort to remove all tangible items in your life that are doing you no good. There may be not too much harm to an occasional drink or even a social cigarette; however, most of us know what is excessive and what is not.

Many people are unhappy in a career for various reasons. We spend most of our time at work and therefore, we need to find a job that interests us and makes us feel fulfilled. You can earn all the money in the world, but if you're not in the correct industry, or you are doing work that you dislike, you will feel uneasy and discontent. These feelings can be tantamount to torture on a daily basis, and it will be no one's fault but your own.

Arrogance and Insecurity

These are classified as obstacles because you put them there yourself—no one else did it to you.

Some people are arrogant because they simply have no regard for ethical conduct or they are trying to hide feelings of insecurity. Others are arrogant because they see themselves as being better than others. Those people who are truly top-notch and world-class do not feel threatened by another's success, beliefs, or actions so they don't need to act arrogantly. Most competent, successful people are very gracious in nature.

Insecurity is caused by a feeling of not being equal to another person or task. It is lack of confidence in one's own ability. Many people are insecure about their career, their family, and other things in life. To feel insecure about certain things is normal; however, you must not lash out and take it out on others. To overcome feelings of insecurity do the following:

- Analyze what exactly is making you feel insecure. Be totally honest with yourself, its okay, the truth is the truth and we all have fears. You don't have to broadcast it to the world, just be honest with yourself.

- Once you have established which fears are making you feel insecure you can start doing those things that you fear. As you face your fears you will gain confidence. You might make a few mistakes and fail a couple of times as you attempt to face and overcome the fears that are making you feel insecure. So what! You are trying to overcome your fears and you should be commended for doing so, as you are observing the **Universal Law of Action and Effect**.

Arrogance and insecurity are obstacles that will prevent growth in life; be mindful of them and overcome them.

I have lived through many topics we discussed in this chapter. My parents separated when I was 10 years old. When I was still a young teenager, I yearned for the past and learned that this yearning was not conducive to contentment. There were financial hardships to some degree; however, I learned that I had the love of my family around me, which made up for more than money could buy. I overcame my lack of education, which was my own fault during my final years at school, by going to technical college and working very hard. I achieved commendations and national awards, which led to further developments in my career. I have learned that negative emotions, such as fear, anger, and bitterness, will only lead to negative results. Negativity is an unhealthy state of mind and can hold us all back: you must learn to control negative emotions, as I did. I have removed all the debris from my life that has caused me unhappiness.

Chapter 16

Harness the Power of Life

Now we will discuss harnessing the power of universal energy—the power of life. We shall discuss seven topics here:

- Four subjects from a spiritual perspective

    1. Identify with the Universe
    2. Believe in Life
    3. Trust Your Inner Guidance
    4. Universal Laws

- Three from a living perspective

    1. Peace, Love, and Fulfillment
    2. Positive Thinking
    3. Action

Identify with the Universe

First of all, identify who you are—a spirit of eternal energy of the universe. Many of us may have a hard time identifying with this idea. Perceiving anything else, other than planet Earth's cultures, religions, and way of life, is hard for people to comprehend and that is understandable.

I want you to conduct a simple exercise here to help you understand and identify with the universe. Close your eyes and imagine yourself in some type of aircraft that can reach the highest atmosphere of the planet and which allows you to view the Earth and outer space. You look from a view port and see the Earth's oceans, landmass, and weather activity. It looks spectacular! You are in awe at our magnificent planet and you're glad it is your home. Now you shift across from one side of the aircraft to the other and look out of another view port. You are now looking 180° from Earth. You are looking into the endless depths of outer space and your eyes cannot count how many stars you see. Ask yourself: "What's out there? How many planets? How many life forms? How many suns?"

You feel excitement, confusion, and curiosity in reviewing this one single dimension. Yes, this is only one single, living dimension out of many in God's universe. Now, do you still think the Earth's cultures, religions, and ways of life are the be all and end all of the universe? I don't think they are—not by a long shot!

Believe in Life

Believe in your life and trust God to help you understand universal learning by having lifetimes of growth and development. Many of you will have religious views and beliefs that will not agree with those written in this book, and there is no problem with that. All I am suggesting is to believe in life.

Have you ever witnessed people from all walks of life, gathered around discussing religion? They seem to get very defensive and aggressive when discussing religion, whether it be their own or someone else's. Have you ever seen what happens when you mention, to people from all walks of life, the subject of past lives and being reincarnated? Their reaction is far more subdued in comparison to your mentioning different religions of the world, and they even pay attention to you when you talk about past lives. Makes you think, doesn't it? Deep within us (our higher minds), there is a place that knows universal knowledge and wisdom.

Now, let me make this perfectly clear once again, you are allowed to worship any form of religion you desire during your lifetime on Earth as per the *Universal Law of Free Will*. All I am stating is that you are a spirit of eternal energy and you will learn God's ways. This is the purpose of your lifetime. Believe in life and believe in God--no matter what happens--because God believes in you, and that is why He gave you the gift of a lifetime to learn and experience.

Enjoy your life and live it to the fullest. If you are gay, straight, rich, poor, man, woman, child—who cares! Just enjoy being alive. Never be ashamed of being gay—that is your business. Do as you please, but harm and offend no others. Don't feel guilty for being rich because of your hard work, and never be ashamed if you are broke because things did not work out for you. As long as you honestly try and give it your best shot, then that is all that is asked of you from God.

Trust Your Inner Guidance

When you're born into this world you are accompanied by spiritual guides. Some refer to these as your guardian angels. Nevertheless, they are here to guide and protect you on your journey of enlightenment and learning.

Often we have feelings of intuition, often described as "gut feelings," about matters of everyday life. As we mentioned earlier in this book, these feelings of intuition and guidance are from your spiritual guides and your own higher mind. Learning to trust your inner guidance means trusting your spiritual guides, as they will guide you for the greater benefit of all concerned— the *Universal Law of Guidance*. You must learn to know the difference between spiritual inner guidance and our human, selfish, egotistical desires. We all know what is right and what is wrong, what is ethical or unethical, and we should certainly know what is legal or illegal.

Trust in your inner guidance. Trust it all the way, as your spiritual guides are with you in your journey until the day you pass on into the other dimension.

Universal Laws

Be aware of the universal laws in your lifetime. These laws are not a set of hard, fast rules that if not obeyed, you will be maligned in the spiritual dimension and be mystically shot or be thrown into a pit of flames.

However, be advised that you live a life of free will and what goes around comes around. For every ounce of unjustifiable harm you inflict on another, the same will be returned to you. All karmic debts you accumulate in this and other lifetimes will be accounted for in one way or another. There is no escaping the universal laws, no matter who you are in this world: king, lawyer, sports star, housewife, or fruit farmer. It matters not, as we are all the same spirits of eternal energy in God's universe and we are all subject to the universal laws.

Have you ever noticed that sometimes people reach certain highs in their lives and they view themselves as untouchable, therefore conducting themselves in whatever fashion they see fit? Then something happens in their life and their world is brought crashing down around them. What goes around comes around. No one who incarnates on Earth is above the universal laws.

The above four topics are viewed from a spiritual perspective. By identifying with the universe, believing in your lifetime, trusting your guidance, and awareness of the universal laws, you will take a major step towards having a successful and fulfilling lifetime in terms of reaching all the predetermined goals and lessons you chose to experience in this living dimension on planet Earth.

Peace, Love, and Fulfillment

During your lifetime, you will be far more comfortable and at ease with yourself and others around you if your goals are to strive for peace and love within you and others, and fulfillment in your lifetime.

You may ask how this is possible in a world full of famine, war, and commercial gain at any cost. However, let me tell you something: there are more good people in this world than you realize. Seek relationships with those who bring peace, love, and fulfillment to your life, and stay away from those who bring nothing but harm and destructive events. You know who these people are, so stay away from them.

In seeking peace in your life, you must not mistake this for letting people dominate you, bully you, and take advantage of you. You must stand up for yourself, no matter what. This business of turning the other cheek is utter rubbish. Do not let people bully you around, no matter who they are: your boss, your father, or your sister. If you do not stand up for yourself you will only know a life of torment, and torment is not a life of peace. Is it? Therefore, in seeking peace, it is sometimes necessary to have some conflict in order to bring about peace. Never, ever look for trouble, but always defend yourself. Be honorable, act with integrity, understanding, and compassion.

Seek love in your life from your family and your friends and even in your career, because love is the golden rule of this universe; without love we are nothing. Those who do not embrace love, give in to hate, which leads to total and utter suffering—the ***Universal Law of Emotional Control***.

Seek fulfillment in your life. You can obtain fulfillment in many forms, such as from your family, friends, and in your career. Fulfillment is an absolute joy in life and should be the goal of all of us. In your heart, you know what will make you fulfilled in life. You know it already, so no one else has to tell you. Therefore, go out in life, make choices, and seek goals that will fulfill you.

Positive Thinking

The saying: "Your thoughts create your reality," is most true—it really is. You must think positively in life. However, do not have an unrealistic sense of reality; being positive about silly and totally unreasonable goals. Most human beings, if not all of us, can achieve anything humanly possible that we want, providing we are willing to work hard and sacrifice for it. Positive thinking creates positive energy and should be encouraged at all times.

Every thought you have creates an energy field. The entire living universe, as well as all other living and spiritual dimensions, are made up of energy— all of it. Therefore, when you think thoughts of fear, anger, and hate, you are creating negative energy. When you surround yourself in negative energy the outcome is generally negative results. Have you ever been around a work colleague who is negative all the time, constantly complaining and emotionally insecure and arrogant? You feel quite uncomfortable around them. That is because they emanate a negative energy field, because their thoughts consist of negative energy—and they do not even have to speak. Your higher mind is sensing the negative vibrational fields being emanated by your work colleague.

When we say do not live in the past and learn to forgive and forget—the *Universal Law of Love*—this is because when you hash over those negative events that happened earlier in your life, you are re-creating the same negative energy frequency field again, which attracts more negative energy and can create even more negative results. Learn to reap the positive from your past events by analyzing and extracting the positive aspects from it. Turn a negative into a positive.

Being positive in life will probably mean that you are trying to achieve goals. By trying to achieve goals in life, you are living and learning. And in case I need to remind you, life is for learning. By being enthusiastic and positive in your goal setting and general conduct in life (you will have your off days too, that's part of being human), you will be surprised at how many things you can achieve in a short amount of time. For example, you may have a list of goals that you wish to achieve over the next three-weeks, such as passing a college exam, repainting your child's room, or taking your children on that road trip you promised them. You will be surprised how quickly your goals will be realized by thinking positively, taking one thing at a time, and doing it properly. However, I must say that even being positive is sometimes not enough to obtain the difficult goals that we sometimes set ourselves in life. Why is this so? Sometimes, the task at hand was not planned well enough, or was just unreasonable in general. Or, in terms of your destiny, perhaps this goal was not meant to be.

You have two simple choices in life: to be positive or to be negative. Look at those people who are positive in nature and compare them to those you know who are negative and pessimistic in their ways, and then ask yourself: "Which should I be?" There is only one answer—be positive!

Action

Whatever you are striving for, and no matter how positive you are, there still remains one important aspect to achieving success and fulfillment in your life, and that is to "just do it!"—the ***Universal Law of Action & Effect***.

Have the belief and conviction that you must in order to create all of your desires, which are a result of positive thinking in your quest for peace, love, and fulfillment in your lifetime. We can read and talk about doing things until we are blue in the face but unless you actually do something, you will learn nothing. You cannot sit on the fence and observe life or meditate and flower power your way around. You must get into the action of life in the 21st Century! Achieve! Achieve! Achieve! Do not let the fear of failure or other people's opinions prevent you from carrying out your dreams. No one wins them all, so you will win some and lose some. There is no shame in failure, providing you give 100%, but there is shame and disappointment when you don't even try.

You chose a lifetime of spiritual learning and participation in the development of planet Earth in the living dimension of God's universe. We all have a karmic responsibility to this world and all life forms in it. Thank God for your lifetime on Earth, embrace it, and do what you need to do in order to seek success and fulfillment in your life. Harness the power of life that is in within you and just do it.

The above three topics are viewed from a living perspective. By striving for peace, love, and fulfillment (being positive and tacking action), you will take another major step towards having a successful and fulfilling lifetime in terms of reaching all the predetermined goals and lessons you chose to experience in this living dimension on planet Earth.

I have identified with the universe and our existence spiritually and physically. I believe in lifetimes and their purpose for spiritual development. I believe in my beloved guides, who have been with me throughout my life. I am aware of the universal laws. However, I am human and not perfect. I am learning to strive for peace, love, and fulfillment in my life. I have learned to think positively and rebuff negative thoughts as much as possible. I have experienced much, so far in my lifetime on the Earth. None of this would have been possible if I didn't do the things I had set out to in my mind, and sub-consciously follow my inner guidance over the last 20 years. I have learned, time and time again, to just do it.

Chapter 17

Success or Failure

First and foremost, you are blessed and honored for incarnating into a life form for growth. You should thank God for the opportunity of a lifetime and thank yourself for attempting to grow. There is no pass or fail grade issued when you have passed on from Earth and are reviewing your lifetime.

Remember, God gives unconditional love, kindness, compassion, and forgiveness for all his spirits. The purpose of a lifetime is to learn! We can review our lifetimes by analyzing these two things:

- What we learned or did not learn from our predetermined lessons.

- What we learned or did not learn from our general conduct in life.

After you return to the heavenly dimension, all universal knowledge will be revealed instantly to you by your guides, and since you are released from the living dimension, so is your higher mind. Your guides will review your pre-life lessons and decide whether these predetermined lessons were learned or have to be repeated again in future lifetimes. Sometimes during review it is a case of, "I knew it! That's where I went awry." And your guides will inform you, "Of course, you knew. We told you, but you did not act."

This state of affairs is fine, because as I have stated numerous times already, the purpose of a lifetime is to live and learn. Only you and your guides know what was to be learned in your lifetime.

However, some information may have been passed on to you in your lifetime via psychic counsel or some other means.

Through your general conduct in life, you will learn and unlearn on a continuous basis and you are subject to The ***Universal Law of Learning***, which states that a spirit's learning challenges will never end. All the lessons of emotions and life experiences that we learn are subject to revocation. The universal laws are in effect for eternity and you must be aware that they all must be followed, regardless of whether you have learned the same lessons in a previous lifetime or not. Let's look at the following example:

- Say you had a lifetime to experience and overcome alcohol addiction. So you chose a lifetime that would lead you to experience and face this challenge. After many years of trying, you finally overcome the addiction and are sober. You now resent and quarrel with those family members around you who socially drink and have fun, because you do not drink socially, as you cannot control your addiction. You become jealous of them and it affects your behavior towards your family members in a negative way. You overcame the experience of addiction, but unlearned the life experience of jealousy. You will now have a lesson on control of jealousy in a future lifetime as a result of your behavior in this lifetime. Although you overcame the actual alcohol addiction, you may have to learn the lesson of addiction again, as you quarreled with others who were innocent and enjoying their lives.

Part 3

Chapter Summary Points

- The Reality of Life on Earth: Mankind has made great advances on Earth, such as healthcare, technology, and space exploration. People's lives are generally healthier and living conditions are improving. However, mankind has still to eradicate very serious problems. But overall, there are more good people than bad ones, more honest nations than tyrannical regimes, and more desire than ever to bring the world together.

- Inner Guidance: Guidance from the spiritual universe and your own higher mind can only help you. In seeking inner guidance, you will open your mind and your life to new possibilities.

- Outer Guidance: We seek outer guidance on a daily basis, whether we realize this or not. Religion, family and friends, and even psychic counsel can serve as good forms of guidance for us.

- Relationships: Our relationships with our families, friends, and people in general can bring us an enormous amount happiness and fulfillment. Relationships are critical in our spiritual development during our lifetime on Earth, as we experience and learn so much because of them.

- Set Goals & Work to Achieve Them: By setting goals for yourself and working towards them, you achieve success and fulfillment in life. Furthermore, you will manifest your lifetime towards your chosen path of learning.

- Overcoming Obstacles: During your lifetime, you are going to have to overcome many obstacles in order to achieve success and fulfillment. Every one of us has challenges we have to face. You have the power of God within you to overcome anything.

- Harness the Power of Life: Harnessing the power of universal energy—the power of life.

Identify with the Universe
Believe in Life
Trust Your Inner Guidance
Universal Laws
Peace, Love, and Fulfillment
Positive Thinking
Action

- Success & Failure: There is no pass or fail grade issued when you have passed on from Earth and are reviewing your lifetime in the spiritual dimension. Your guides will review your pre-life lessons and decide whether these predetermined lessons were learned or have to be repeated again in future lifetimes.

Part 4

Closing Statement

For many of you the concept of universal learning is foreign and somewhat difficult to comprehend, this is understandable as it is simply the reality of reading and understanding something new and different. Some may say, "This universal learning thinking is relatively new and has no track record." Please be advised that the concepts of eternal life, reincarnation, superior being, universal energy, and laws that govern the stars were present in most early Earth cultures in various formats long before popular modern day faiths such as Christianity and Islam were established.

I stated earlier in the book that acknowledging universal learning does not require you to alter your present belief system. "Why is this so?" you may ask. All life revolves around universal learning, no matter what religion or faith you belong to; it matters not if you're a Christian, Muslim, or Jew. "Why doesn't it matter?" you may ask further. Why does it have to matter what Earth belief you have? The universal laws and universal energy are here in this living dimension irrespective of what religion or faith you belong to and they operate with or without you, doing your faith or religion no harm or disrespect.

I want you to read carefully and ask yourself who is responsible for all of this?

- Who made the universe of this living dimension
- Dreams
- Déjà vu
- Feelings of past lives
- Emotions

- Your feelings of intuition
- Psychic clairvoyance
- The inner belief that most of us have, of something more than what's on planet Earth

Take a look at the cover page of the book. Just look at it. Look at it! This cover page is not fiction; it is reality! Look at all the stars, the Earth—magnificent! This is where you are right now. Who created all of this? What binds it together? The superior spirit—God—did, with **universal energy** which binds all the stars and planets in this dimension together.

The **universal laws** that pertain to this living dimension are given to you by God to help and guide you in the lifetimes of universal learning that you undertake in this living dimension.

May you achieve happiness, success, and fulfillment within your goals of universal learning in your lifetime on planet Earth.

References & Inspiration

- Heavenly Insight on Love, Life & Dreams by Camille Starr, Leona Mayers, and Marlene Scanlon Camille Publications ISBN 0-9628442-0-9 www.leonamayers. com

- Creative Visualization audio CD by Shati Gwain New World Library www.newworldlibrary.com

- Guided Meditations audio CD by Bodhipaksa www. wildmind.org

- Stephen Adair www.lifeandsoulcoachingco.co.uk